LA GRA
ILLUSION

CINÉ-FILES: The French Film Guides
Series Editor: Ginette Vincendeau

From the pioneering days of the Lumière brothers' Cinématographe in 1895, France has been home to perhaps the most consistently vibrant film culture in the world, producing world-class directors and stars, and a stream of remarkable movies, from popular genre films to cult avant-garde works. Many of these have found a devoted audience outside France, and the arrival of DVD is now enabling a whole new generation to have access to contemporary titles as well as the great classics of the past.

The **Ciné-Files French Film Guides** build on this welcome new access, offering authoritative and entertaining guides to some of the most significant titles, from the silent era to the early twenty-first century. Written by experts in French cinema, the books combine extensive research with the author's distinctive, sometimes provocative perspective on each film. The series will thus build up an essential collection on great French classics, enabling students, teachers and lovers of French cinema both to learn more about their favourite films and make new discoveries in one of the world's richest bodies of cinematic work.

Ginette Vincendeau

Published Ciné-Files:
Alphaville (Jean-Luc Godard, 1965) – Chris Darke
Amelie (Jean-Pierre Jeunet, 2001) – Isabelle Vanderschelden
Casque d'or (Jacques Becker, 1952) – Sarah Leahy
Cléo de 5 à 7 (Agnès Varda, 1962) – Valerie Orpen
La Grande Illusion (Jean Renoir, 1937) – Martin O'Shaughnessy
La Haine (Mathieu Kassovitz, 1995) – Ginette Vincendeau
La Règle du jeu (Jean Renoir, 1939) – Keith Reader
La Reine Margot (Patrice Chereau, 1994) – Julianne Pidduck
Le Corbeau (Henri-Georges Clouzot, 1943) – Judith Mayne
Les Diaboliques (Henri-Georges Clouzot, 1955) – Susan Hayward
Nikita (Luc Besson, 1990) – Susan Hayward
Rififi (Jules Dassin, 1955) – Alastair Phillips
Un chien andalou (Luis Buñuel, 1929) – Elza Adamowicz

LA GRANDE ILLUSION

(Jean Renoir, 1937)

Martin O'Shaughnessy

I.B. TAURIS

LONDON · NEW YORK

Published in 2009 by I.B.Tauris & Co Ltd

6 Salem Road, London W2 4BU

175 Fifth Avenue, New York NY 10010

www.ibtauris.com

Distributed in the United States and Canada Exclusively by Palgrave Macmillan

175 Fifth Avenue, New York NY 10010

ISBN: 978 1 84885 057 6

A full CIP record for this book is available from the British Library

A full CIP record is available from the Library of Congress

Library of Congress Catalog Card Number: available

Printed and bound in India by Thomson Press India Ltd

from camera-ready copy edited and supplied by the author

Contents

Acknowledgements

My warm thanks go: to Ginette Vincendeau, the series editor, for all her support and advice; to Christopher Faulkner and Olivier Curchod for their generous willingness to discuss ideas and share their tremendous knowledge of Renoir; to staff at the Bibliothèque du Film in Paris and the Lilly library of the University of Indiana for their invaluable assistance; to Pat FitzGerald, Jayne Hill, Philippa Brewster and David Oswald for helping to bring the book to fruition; to my wife and children for their support and understanding and for the sense of perspective they helped me hold on to.

Introduction

Made by France's greatest director, Jean Renoir, at the very height of his powers, *La Grande Illusion* is widely considered one of the very finest French films, the world's greatest pacifist film and one of the most important war films. Premiered on 8 June 1937 and opened to the public a day later at the Marivaux cinema in Paris, *La Grande Illusion* was an immediate critical and popular success and number one French box office hit for the year. Ex-servicemen's associations sponsored its release around the country in the autumn of that same year, while to commemorate 11 November, Armistice Day for the Great War, it was specially shown in 52 cinemas.[1] It was also a major international hit at a time when the reputation of French cinema as a whole ran very high. One of several films representing France at the Venice film festival in 1937, it seemed set to win the Mussolini Cup, the major prize. Because such a triumph might have been more than a little awkward in a fascist Italy far from committed to peace, it was deemed more expedient to award it a specially invented trophy, the international Jury Cup, for the best artistic ensemble.[2] It was a major success in the United States, running for twenty-six weeks in New York in 1938, and was voted best picture that same year by the National Board of Review and best foreign film at the New York Film Critics Circle awards. In 1939, it was the first foreign film ever nominated for the Oscar for best picture, although it failed to win. Mussolini reportedly much admired the film, although it was blocked from general release in Italy until a reciprocal deal was made in 1938.[3] Goebbels apparently labelled it 'cinematic enemy number one'.[4] It was unsurprisingly banned in Nazi Germany. In contrast, when it was privately screened for President and Mrs Roosevelt at the White House on 11 October 1938, the President is said to have declared that it was a film that should be seen in all the democracies of the world.[5]

The coming of the Second World War unsurprisingly caused *La Grande Illusion* to disappear from most European cinema screens. Censored by the French authorities even before the German invasion of 1940, it was predictably banned by the Nazi occupier with copies being gathered in for destruction. It was nonetheless Renoir's inevitable calling card when he sought to establish himself in Hollywood.[6] The Liberation of France and defeat of fascism reopened the possibility of European release, something towards which Renoir energetically worked despite his American exile, but something which was initially blocked by censors due to what were deemed to be problematic aspects of the film. A censored version was finally released on 28 August 1946 at the Normandie cinema in Paris and was again a major box-office hit, despite arousing fierce critical debate. The year 1958 was to doubly consolidate its enormous reputation. A painstakingly restored version was again a great public success in France, while 117 film historians from around the world voted it one of the twelve best films ever made, the only French film to achieve this honour.[7] Of 105 votes given to Renoir's works, 75 went to *La Grande Illusion*, a measure of its pre-eminence at that time. Although it has been displaced as Renoir's most celebrated film by *La Règle du jeu* since the 1960s, it is still rightly grouped among the works that confirm his status as one of the greatest directors in the history of film. For a long time, the available version of the film was that restored under Renoir's guidance using a duplicate negative in the 1950s. Thankfully, however, and rather bizarrely, the original negative turned up in vaults of the Toulouse *Cinémathèque*, having been passed on by the Soviet Union which had presumably shipped it back to Moscow after removing it from the *Reichfilmarchiv* in Berlin alongside other films confiscated after the war.[8] A restored and beautifully clear print is now available and easily obtained on DVD.

While not seeking to provide a definitive account of the film – were such a thing possible – to match the apparently definitive print now available, this study will seek to provide a rounded exploration of it, covering its sources, different creative inputs into it and its complex production and reception histories. Considerable attention will predictably be paid to form (mise-en-scène, camera, editing, sound and music, narrative construction) although the book will never be narrowly formalist, as the film's formal choices are clearly inseparable from the kind of intervention it seeks to make in its

troubled times. The overt modernist brilliance and sharp shifts of tone of
La Règle du jeu tend to attract much comment on its style. Less *obviously*
brilliant than *La Règle*, *La Grande Illusion* nonetheless finds Renoir at the
absolute peak of his form and is a classic example of his 1930s film-making.
Similarly, while some of the casting of *La Règle* might seem a little dubious,
La Grande Illusion catches some excellent yet highly contrasting performers
– Erich von Stroheim, Jean Gabin, Pierre Fresnay, Dita Parlo, Carette – on top
form. Attention will be paid to the complex interplay of performance styles
that their combination permits, as well as to how Renoir inflects the screen
persona that each brings with them. But again, consideration of stars and
their use will not be allowed to take us away from the film's politics. Issues of
war and peace, of nation and class, of ethnicity and gender, of social struggle
and historical possibility are central to the film and will be given their due
place. What will also be a central concern is *La Grande Illusion*'s status as a
classic example of political cinema. It is often thought that political cinema
has to distance itself from mainstream narrative cinema if it is not to betray its
political intent. *La Grande Illusion* shows that it is (or, at least, *was*) possible
to make a highly intelligent political film rooted in popular culture, provided
of course that the popular itself is reworked from within by a politics.

Notes

1   Curchod, Olivier, *La Grande Illusion* (Paris, 2005), p. 16.
2   See Kelly, Andrew, *Cinema and the Great War* (London, 1997), p. 114 and
    Bergan, Ronald, *Jean Renoir: Projections of Paradise* (London, 1992), p. 179. The
    Mussolini Cup instead went to Julien Duvivier's *Un Carnet de bal*, a film about
    missed romantic opportunities and thus a far less controversial choice.
3   Italian distribution was reportedly obtained in exchange for French release of
    Carmine Gallone's 1937 propagandist fascist costume epic, *Scipio, the African*
    (Priot, Franck, 'La Grande Illusion: histoire du film en dix chapitres', *Archives* 70
    (February 1997), pp. 16–17).
4   Kelly, *Cinema and the Great War*, p. 114.
5   Faulkner, Christopher, *The Social Cinema of Jean Renoir* (Princeton, 1986),
    p. 105.
6   See Vitanza, Elizabeth, 'Another Grand Illusion: Jean Renoir's first year in
    America', *The Film Journal*, www.thefilmjournal.com/issue12/renoir.html
    (consulted 31/3/2008).
7   *La Grande Illusion* came in fifth, behind Eisenstein's *Battleship Potemkin*,
    Chaplin's *Gold-Rush*, de Sica's *Bicycle Thieves* and Dreyer's *The Passion of Joan of*

Arc. See Viry-Babel, Roger, 'La Grande Illusion de Jean Renoir', *Les Cahiers de la Cinémathèque*, 18–19 (Spring 1976), p. 59.

8   On the film's restoration, see Aubert, Michelle, 'La Grande Illusion de Jean Renoir: histoire d'une restauration', *Archives* 70 (February 1997), pp. 27–28.

1 Contexts

All films arise out of the complex coming together of broad socio-historical and narrower film-industrial contexts. They are also inevitably collective productions even if we sometimes talk about them as if only the director mattered. Because of this *La Grande Illusion* needs a multi-layered contextualisation. It can profitably be located in the career of its director in a way that will bring out its stylistic or thematic relationship with his other works. Yet, it must also be seen in terms of the interaction of director, performers and other creative personnel in a way inevitably conditioned by the particular mode of organisation of the French film industry in the 1930s. Finally, it needs to be seen as a product of its troubled period and as part of French society's evolving reflexion on the slaughter of the First World War even as fascism and another war threatened. If these different contextual layers cannot be collapsed into each other, nor can they can be kept neatly separate. Renoir's career, for example, was inevitably shaped by both the nature and practices of the French cinema industry and by broader socio-political factors while the war itself was not an impersonal contextual factor but something that had directly impacted on him and his family.

A director and his two careers

As is well known, Jean Renoir was the son of Auguste, the great painter. One might have expected him to have turned to painting or one of the other arts as a career. Instead, in February 1913, he enlisted in the First Regiment of Dragoons and had qualified as an officer by the time war started in August 1914. Although technically a horseman, he soon found himself in the trenches like other cavalrymen. In April 1915 he received a leg wound that turned gangrenous. Saved by a skilled doctor, he would nonetheless limp for the rest of his life. His mother Aline, a sick woman, rushed to his bedside, stayed to see him recover, but died soon after returning home. After a period of convalescence, Renoir returned to the war, first as an observer taking photographs from slow-moving reconnaissance planes, then as a pilot, until a bad landing aggravated his leg wound and put him out of action for the duration.[1] The war also left its mark on his brother, Pierre, leaving him with a badly damaged arm. Renoir would call upon this wartime experience to underline the authenticity of what is seen in *La Grande Illusion*. He liked to point out that it is his flying jacket that Gabin is seen wearing in the film.[2] If his experience in reconnaissance can be seen as an unconventional introduction to photography, his injuries and the enforced rest they ensured gave him the chance to indulge a passion for watching films, especially the American ones that, with much French production out of action, now dominated cinema screens. Within a few years he would be making his own films.

The silent period was a distinctly uneven part of Renoir's career. It saw him direct films ranging from the visually experimental but melodramatic *La Fille de l'eau* (1924), through the avant-gardist *Charleston* (1926) and the colonialist commission *Le Bled* (1930), to the barrack-room comedy, *Tire-au-flanc* (1928).[3] Even a dedicated auteurist critic *should* struggle to find a consistent outlook across these films. Their only really consistent feature is a concern with formal and technical experiment.

Sound was to transform French cinema in general and Renoir's work in particular. Because sound technology made films much more expensive to make and show, it pushed the French industry towards more commercial work and discouraged the kind of experimentation that had marked some of the filmic output of the 1920s including Renoir's films. Driven to look for ready-made scripts to fill the need for dialogue, Renoir turned, along with much of French cinema, towards theatrical adaptation, making three successful boulevard comedies into films: *On purge bébé* (1931); *Boudu sauvé des eaux* (1932); *Chotard et Cie* (1933). These works were interspersed with three adaptations of novels: *La Chienne* (1931), *La Nuit du Carrefour* (1932) and *Madame Bovary* (1933). Because most of these early sound films are gently or sharply critical of the pretensions and self-repression of the bourgeoisie, it becomes a little easier to make a case for thematic consistency across Renoir's output. However, because all drew on literary genres (the boulevard comedy, the realist novel) that routinely satirized or dissected the bourgeoisie, one should hesitate to attribute any consistency to a consistent directorial project. What they do show however is how quickly Renoir came to terms with the demands of sound and began to develop the formal repertoire that would come to full maturity in his films of the later 1930s, notably in *La Grande Illusion*.

On purge bébé, Renoir's first sound film, is the closest he ever came to filmed theatre. Remarkably tame when set against the visual experimentation of the silent years, it is shot in a transparently theatrical décor with no opening onto the outer world. The only technical aspect of it that Renoir tended to recall in later years was the use of the sound of a real toilet flushing, early evidence of his preference for acoustic realism. From only a year later, *Boudu sauvé des eaux* is a remarkably different piece of work. Although its interiors are shot in constructed decors (as they would consistently be in Renoir's 1930s films), there is already great use made of the kind of composition in depth that would be such an essential feature of his mature pre-war work. The film's preference for location shooting of exteriors is shared by Renoir's adaptations of novels in the early 1930s. Made a year after *Boudu*, the likeable but unremarkable *Chotard et Cie* confirms the existence of an emergent style. It is repeatedly characterised by a freely panning and tracking camera and in-depth staging that links its different spaces.

Toni (1934) signalled a shift in Renoir's career. Shot on location in the South of France, it moved him sharply towards contemporary issues and working class themes. Locating itself amongst a range of largely Mediterranean migrants, quarry workers, charcoal burners and peasants, it set itself firmly on the side of its Italian immigrant hero. It thus refused any narrow or closed definition of Frenchness and national belonging even if it did not entirely escape stereotypes of hot-blooded latins.[4] At a time of virulent xenophobia in France, it suggested a deliberate taking of position that, alongside its admirable image of worker solidarity, suggested emergent political commitment.

Renoir's political involvement was confirmed by his cinematic and extra-cinematic activities during the period of the Popular Front when he became France's leading left-wing film-maker. He confirmed his radicalisation with *Le Crime de Monsieur Lange* (1935), a film made with the heavy involvement of the radical theatre troupe, *Le Groupe Octobre*, and with leftist anarchist poet and legendary script-writer Jacques Prévert. It tells the story of a print-workers' co-operative that arises after the forced departure of a capitalist boss. The fact that the co-operative reaches out to embrace all those who live around the courtyard where it is based is one factor that has meant that it has often been seen as typical of the values of a Popular Front that sought to build a broad and inclusive anti-fascist alliance. Yet, at the same time, the hero's murder of the capitalist and the film's sideswipes at the clergy and the military demonstrate a radicalism often attributed to the influence of the *Groupe Octobre* and Prévert rather than the director. Whatever the case may have been, Renoir's next project confirmed his political commitment beyond any doubt as he was to supervise the collective production of *La Vie est à nous*, a propaganda film made for the French Communist Party in the run up to the 1936 elections that would bring the Popular Front of which they were a part to power. While *La Vie's* stylistic diversity and eclectic mix of documentary, newsreel and fictionalised episodes underscore the collective nature of its production, some parts clearly bear Renoir's hallmark features of the period, notably composition in depth, long takes, connection of different spaces and a highly mobile camera. These same features had of course been displayed to full advantage and taken to virtuoso lengths in *Le Crime de Monsieur Lange* whose courtyard set, as André Bazin, the great French film theorist, notes, invited the kind of tracking and panning movements that are so typical of Renoir's work at that time.[5]

Bazin suggests more generally that what distinguishes the mise-en-scène of the pre-war Renoir is the way in which his films constantly activate off-screen space. Renoir recognises that the frame is not so much a window on the world as a mask, so that what we cannot see is as important as what we can. While we only view what the camera permits, we are also constantly made aware that what we cannot see nonetheless continues to exist. Rather than giving us the impression that the action has been staged for the frame and has no existence beyond it, the action in a Renoir film seems to pass through the frame and to exist before and after it. The primary way that this is achieved is through the mobility of the tracking and panning camera and through long takes, stylistic choices that together mean that constant reframing tends to substitute itself for cuts, so preserving the integrity and continuity of the filmed 'world'. The natural extension of the lateral mobility of the camera is the depth of composition of the typical Renoir shot, a feature which ensures that actors are solidly located in the spatial context of their actions rather than being isolated on a single plane and detached from their surroundings.[6]

While Bazin encapsulates Renoir's mature 1930s style with typical brilliance, there is a danger that he may push us to see it in terms of a purely ontological realism, one that resists the fragmentation of the filmed world by editing and underscores the fundamental interconnectedness of the real. Christopher Faulkner's work has provided a vital supplement to such a view by showing how Renoir's realism is a social one that works to bring class relations to the fore. When Renoir's camera connects different spaces through composition in depth or tracking and panning, it locates actions in their social context and connects different social groups, highlighting their interaction and probing the nature of their inter-relation.[7] Renoir's style of the middle and later 1930s did not spring up from nowhere in response to his political commitment. As I have shown, elements of it can be traced back to the beginning of the sound period or earlier. But what happened, about the time of the Popular Front, is that Renoir's increasingly assured style and the content of his films aligned in a tremendously productive way. Even as the films took on a new awareness of the contemporary context and of the social struggles associated with it, the style found, one might say, its reason to exist.

Renoir's involvement in *La Vie est à nous* underlined how he had become a Communist fellow traveller; that is, someone who was close to the party without being a member. This proximity was underscored by the cinema column that he began writing for the Communist evening paper, *Ce soir*, edited at the time by the great ex-Surrealist poet Louis Aragon.[8] It was also emphasised by the leading role he took in Ciné-Liberté, an association that was a bold but short-lived Popular Front driven attempt to move towards a radically different cinema industry organised along co-operative lines and outside of the capitalist economy.[9] Initially secretary of the association, Renoir became the chair of its governing body and was the natural choice to direct its flagship project, *La Marseillaise,* a film which was to be funded by public subscription, underscoring the desired break with commercial production and the values associated with it. Originally intended to celebrate the Popular Front's shared purpose, the film unwittingly underlined its coming apart because, as it neared completion, only the Communists and the Communist inspired union federation, the CGT, remained on board, with the latter providing the extras for the crowd scenes.[10] Public subscription failed to provide sufficient funds for the film and it had to retreat to more conventionally commercial means.

Merely to see *La Marseillaise* as the expression of a defeat would be to overlook its radical intent. Telling the story of how representatives of Marseilles brought the French revolutionary anthem north to the capital and onwards to the great French victory at Valmy, Renoir's film was part of a broader attempt by the Popular Front to reclaim the symbols and the history of nation from the nationalist right in the run up to the 150th anniversary of the beginning of the Revolution of 1789. The film invited the French public to make sense of their contemporary experience by drawing on the revolutionary tradition, with its preference for the radical egalitarian Revolution of 1792 over the moderate one of 1789 being a restatement of revolutionary vigour at a time when the Popular Front was flagging. It was being prepared even as *La Grande Illusion* was being shot. If it would be a mistake simply to see the two films as dimensions of the same project, not least because of *La Grande Illusion*'s more conventional production context, there are good reasons for thinking about the two together. While the events they deal with – the Revolution and the Great War – are more than a century apart, both seek to connect past and present struggles while mobilising French Republican traditions. More specifically, of course, both give an important place to the 'Marseillaise,' an anthem clearly central to the eponymous film but which also occurs, as we shall see, at a key turning point of *La Grande Illusion*. The two films can be joined to *La Règle du jeu* (1939) to form a revolutionary triptych, as long as one remembers, of course, that in the latter film the revolutionary tradition is a structuring absence, something whose disappearance means that all hope of progressive change has disappeared from a society no longer able to renew itself and torn between destructive repetition and fascistic regression.[11] It is no accident that the film's chief location is a *château*, that symbol of pre-revolutionary France. *La Règle du jeu* confirms the burying of the political optimism that came into Renoir's film-making with the emergence of the Popular Front and shows a France heading blindly towards war while its inhabitants pursue their own frivolous and selfish concerns.

Taken together, *La Grande Illusion*, *La Marseillaise* and *La Règle du jeu* remind us that the Popular Front did not merely open Renoir's works to the contemporary world and the struggles that structured it, it also opened them up to history, to a sense that the world could change for better or for worse. It is therefore vital to analyse how the possibility of change is embedded within their narrative, characterisation, décor and mise-en-scène. Renoir's films of the period are not simply shot, as has often been remarked, in 'deep space' (with the full depth of the image being mobilised to bring social groups and contrasting spaces into contact), they are also shot in 'deep time' as the struggles between different socio-historical possibilities are played out across their story space. The same awareness of potential change also runs through another film from the same period, *Les Bas-fonds* (1937). If it begins by showing a world apparently characterised by fixed social roles and predictable destinies, it has shown by its conclusion that locations, costumes and even the shape of narratives in which characters find themselves are mutable.[12]

Les Bas-fonds was one of three films that Renoir made with Jean Gabin during the Popular Front period, alongside *La Grande Illusion* and the noir classic *La Bête humaine* (1938). Gabin was then emerging as *the* major French star of the era. The fact that Renoir was repeatedly able to work with him underlines both his high reputation as a director and his desire to make films that reached out for a large, popular audience. If popular cinema tends to avoid overt political comment because it inevitably runs the risk of alienating elements of the large audience that it seeks to assemble, the Popular Front period briefly opened up the possibility of a popular, political cinema. Renoir's films showed that there are different ways to be popular *and* political. One way, something aspired to by Ciné-Liberté, was to involve the common people or the workers as active partners in film production. Another was to consistently make the 'ordinary' people the central protagonists of the drama, rather than the bourgeoisie as in the films of the earlier 1930s. A third was to address a popular audience by figuring its concerns and by speaking to it in the idiom of popular cinema. Thus, for example, *Le Crime de Monsieur Lange* used popular genres (the crime drama, the love story, the western), popular song and working class characters as a way of bringing a political story to a popular audience. But at the same time, each element needed to be worked upon to open it up to a progressive politics. Although the film was not a great box office success, it indicated the direction *La Grande Illusion* would need to take to bring its progressive vision to a wide public.

Cast and creative personnel

In the United States, the 1930s were the heyday of the Hollywood studio system with major studios dominating production, distribution and exhibition and with actors and technicians tied down by permanent studio contracts. It looked as if France might move in some similar directions in the early 1930s, with Pathé and Gaumont as the two major studios. However, their own mismanagement and the broader economic slump prevented such a development. The French system remained fragmented and under-financed and productions were typically put together as individual packages with cast and creative personnel brought together for each project.[13] Clearly, this system had advantages and disadvantages. If it meant that finance had to be put together on a film by film basis, it also meant that French directors had much more freedom to assemble their cast and crew than their Hollywood equivalents. An examination of Renoir's 1930s filmography shows that his work was no exception to this more general pattern.

Almost without exception, Renoir's 1930s films have different producers, with the only exceptions being *On purge bébé* and *La Chienne* both made with Braunberger and Richebé at the start of the decade and *Une Partie de campagne* which Braunberger co-produced in 1936. In contrast, the creative personnel of Renoir's films show a considerable degree of stability. Joseph de Bretagne joined Renoir as sound engineer on *La Chienne* and worked on another six films during the decade. Joseph Kosma composed music for

Toni in 1934 and went on to work on another five films, or six if one includes *Une Partie de campagne* to which the score was added when it was edited after the Second World War. Jean Bachelet's first camera credit with Renoir was on his first film, *La Fille de l'eau*. His name reappeared five times in the silent era and another four times in the 1930s. Claude Renoir, Jean's nephew, made his first appearance behind the camera for *Toni* and went on to work on some of Renoir's major 1930s films. Renoir's companion for much of the 1930s, Marguerite Houlle-Renoir, co-edited *La Chienne* and edited all the subsequent 1930s films. Jean Castanier designed the set of three of the 1930s films and Eugène Lourié five. Renoir himself is given writing credits for all of the films of the period, having collaborated twice with the great scriptwriter Charles Spaak and been supported several times by his close German friend Carl Koch. Jacques Becker, later a notable director in his own right, was Renoir's assistant for much of the 1930s. It is in the context of this impressive stability that one should seek to explain Renoir's ability to develop and maintain a consistent style in his 1930s films. Many of the same creative personnel would of course appear on the credits of *La Grande Illusion*: Spaak, Houlle-Renoir, Claude Renoir, Lourié, Kosma, de Bretagne, Koch, Becker.

Renoir's cast lists from the period predictably show much less stability but some favourite names do recur, sometimes on several occasions. Michel Simon, the great comic actor, worked in four films from 1928 to 1932. Jean's brother Pierre starred in two early 1930s films as well as playing the ill-fated Louis XVI in *La Marseillaise*. Some of the main players in *Toni* were also to reappear in *La Marseillaise*. Several actors enjoyed 'mini-series' with Renoir in the later 1930s. Jean Gabin, as we have noted, starred in three films from 1936 to 1938. Marcel Dalio, given his first starring role in *La Grande Illusion*, would enjoy similar prominence in *La Règle du jeu*. Julien Carette would appear in four films, starting with *La Grande Illusion*. This reappearance of performers naturally reinforced the possibility of dialogue between the films. However, if some of the stars of *La Grande Illusion* (Gabin, Carette, Dalio) were or would become Renoir regulars, others stars were one-off figures but would have a significant impact on the film. Erich von Stroheim and Dita Parlo, both late additions, caused major reworkings of the script. Pierre Fresnay, a noted stage actor, was not the first choice to play the aristocratic Edmond de Boeldieu, although he made the part his own.

The original choice was another celebrated theatrical star, the great Louis Jouvet. Had Jouvet been able to take the role, it would have created another Renoir 'mini-series', given his performance as the baron in *Les Bas-fonds* and his impressive cameo in *La Marseillaise*. Stars like Gabin, Stroheim, Fresnay or Parlo did not of course come to Renoir without a considerable baggage. It is therefore important to consider their existing personae and how they shaped the film but also, crucially, how Renoir moulded them to his broader project in line with its underlying politics.

There can be little doubt that Jean Gabin was the leading French film star of the latter half of the 1930s. Although he was originally a comic music-hall singer, his screen persona was that of the tough but warm ordinary man as embodied in a series of proletarian or underworld roles from the early 1930s onwards.[14] His dominant 1930s persona began to emerge as early as films such as the 'Diva' movie, *Paris-Béguin* (Genina, 1931) in which he was both a tough gangster and a vulnerable man brought down by women. His later characters would tend to reproduce that same mixture of toughness and vulnerability, romance and virility, a combination that explains his ability to appeal to a mixed audience. The same mixture of traits was supported by his physique; a stocky, powerful body on the one hand, fair hair and clear, striking blue eyes on the other.[15] His persona was to firm up around the middle of the decade with Julien Duvivier's foreign legion drama, *La Bandera* (1935), in which, having joined the legion to escape the consequences of a murder he has committed in Paris, Gabin's character dies just as he achieves some sort of atonement through military service. Ensuing 'poetic realist' classics by Duvivier, Carné and Grémillon would end with Gabin either dead or exiled or both. Although Gabin's characters were sometimes either career criminals or guilty of crimes, they were also typically likeable because of their honesty and loyalty. These same qualities were associated with his performances of proletarians. Associated with down-to-earth, ordinary Frenchmen, his persona had strong connotations of authenticity. This quality was partially rooted in his famous performance style. Despite his beginnings in music-hall, his screen style was marked by poise, understatement and naturalistic speech. In a film such as Duvivier's *Pépé le Moko* (1937), for example, the authenticity of the Gabin performance is confirmed by the theatrical acting style of those around him. Proletarian authenticity was also suggested by his on and off-screen association with popular sports such as boxing, cycling or football.[16]

Gabin's persona was not simply that of the ordinary man, it was that of the ordinary *Frenchman*. Frenchness was embedded in his characters and off-screen image in a range of ways. His characters were typically popular Parisians, an identification authenticated by their accent and his own Parisian roots. Yet, like many French people, he also had a rural background having been brought up by grandparents in a little village. This background was activated in a number of his films. If Paris, the capital, often stands in metonymically for France, rural France, or 'deep' France (*'la France profonde'*) as it is known, serves to ground a rooted, unchanging sense of Frenchness.[17] Doubly French therefore, Gabin's national belonging was underscored and racialised in films where he was pitted against foreigners. *La Bandera* saw him fighting Moroccan rebels or *'salopards'* ('bastards') as the film labelled them. *Pépé le Moko* pitted him against a devious Algerian policeman. While Gabin's characters were often cast as the centre of French community, through association, for example, with places of popular sociability such as the bistrot, the racialisation of the persona tended to imply that this 'cosy' community was exclusively white.[18]

Gabin's star image clearly had much to offer Renoir while at the same time bearing a negative baggage that would need to be dealt with. If it is remarkable how much of his image passed relatively intact into Renoir's Popular Front films, it is also significant how the director inflected his persona. Maréchal, the character Gabin plays in *La Grande Illusion*, is in many ways a typical Gabin vehicle that activates core elements of the star's mythology. Pre-war, Maréchal has been a mechanic in a factory and thus part of the working class elite. He is from Paris, but can call on memories of feeding his grandfather's cows. He is vigorously masculine, as seen in the escape sequence, yet also tender and indeed romantic, as evidenced by the film's love story. As in his other films, he is committed to the group and states more than once that what he is doing is for 'les copains', his mates. As the film begins, he is singing along nostalgically to a gramophone recording of 'Frou frou' by Fréhel, the great *chanteuse réaliste*, thus reminding us of Gabin's stage career while further underlining the character's popular roots. His performance is typically understated, as one would expect, yet he also gives vent to two typical Gabin rages when he loses control in solitary confinement and when a repressed anti-Semitism breaks through the surface under pressure. Yet the anti-Semitism and the song point to some of the potential problems with the inherited Gabin persona and to some of the political work that Renoir needed to do upon it. Gabin's associations with popular community and with loyalty can clearly be connected to key leftist virtues of equality and solidarity. But, as we noted, this community was sometimes implicitly or explicitly racialised. Forcing the character's anti-Semitism to the surface, as Renoir does in *La Grande Illusion*, is a way of confronting the issue. The singing of 'Frou frou' reminds us of a nostalgia often connected with Gabin's persona and frequently activated by songs (as in *La Bandera* and *Pépé le Moko*). Renoir's film acknowledges this nostalgic dimension but will work to open it onto the future and the possibility of progressive change. Gabin's character is routinely trapped by his social status, by the past, by a fate in the face of which he is often strangely passive. Maréchal, in contrast, is an activist character so that the film is not merely an escape drama in the banal sense but is also a tale of escape from imprisoning circumstances and attitudes. In the same way as *Les Bas-fonds* rescues the Gabin persona from the picturesque lower depths to which he was so often condemned by a series of 'Poetic Realist' classics, *La Grande Illusion* rescues him from the prison houses of nationalism, racism and mono-lingualism.

Julien Carette who plays Cartier, the music hall performer, is worth considering alongside Gabin, because he is, to some extent, a parodic double of the star. Like Gabin, Carette is a stereotypical Parisian performer with clearly signalled popular roots, not least because of his accent and 'cheeky chappie' chirpiness or '*gouaille*'. But while Gabin's performances are marked by restraint and seriousness, Carette's are typified by comedy and verbal and physical excess. Although he is only present in the first prison camp in *La Grande Illusion*, his larger-than-life presence there plays a key role in establishing the mood of that part of the film, lightening and complicating its drama with a dose of frivolity and disorder. Yet Carette-Cartier's carnivalesque presence also has a potential political edge to it. His undisciplined body and disrespectful address is a challenge to the order and hierarchy of the prison camp where the French find themselves. A challenge that remains, of course, at the symbolic level, as evidenced in the sequence where he does a little, mocking jig to a German military march and ostentatiously pretends he is about to step through the wire.

As the aristocratic career officer, Edmond de Boeldieu, Pierre Fresnay gives one of the film's towering performances. More a star actor than an out-and-out star, his 1930s persona is less sharply defined than that of Gabin or Carette. A classically trained stage performer, he initially achieved cinema stardom as Marius in Pagnol's classic Marseilles trilogy, a role he had already played on stage, having quickly mastered the meridional accent. However, his clear, incisive diction meant he more often played middle or upper class types, often in roles of authority. He was thus ideally suited to play de Boeldieu, even if he was not first choice for the role. His presence allows Renoir to play off his clipped, upper class tones against Gabin's proletarian Parisian to emphasise the class differences between them. His theatrical background is turned to positive advantage to underline how the aristocrat *performs* his social role while the more naturalistic Gabin simply seems to be his. He is not a humourless character, but humour in his case takes the form of irony and distances him from the situations he finds himself in. In contrast, Carette's proletarian humour is physical, vulgar and invites shared enjoyment and involvement.

Alongside Carette, Dalio was one of the fine supporting actors that so characterised classical French cinema. Unlike Carette however and despite being born in Paris, the Jewish Dalio was often called upon to play non-French and sometimes, but not inevitably, untrustworthy characters in exotic locations. A rabbi in Duvivier's *Le Golem* (1935) he was the treacherous l'Arbi in the same director's *Pépé le Moko*, an Abyssinian in *Les Perles de la couronne* (1937), a Maltese in Pierre Chenal's *La Maison du Maltais* (1938) and a mercenary in Christian Jaque's far Eastern adventure *Les Pirates du rail* (1937). Slight of stature, with black wavy hair and sallow skin, Dalio's features lent themselves towards this kind of casting. The practice whereby someone deemed to look 'exotic' could play almost any non-western role was routine in French cinema as in the Hollywood of the day. As with his other leads, Renoir both used and reworked Dalio's existing persona in *La Grande Illusion*. Simultaneously foregrounding his Jewishness, his apparently foreign roots *and* his Frenchness, he used the character to problematise easy assumptions about fixed national belonging and ethnic frontiers.

Dalio's pairing with Erich von Stroheim is a fascinating one. A naturalised American with Austrian roots, Stroheim was one of the legendary directors of early cinema until the cost of his films made it impossible for him to find backers. He initially worked with another legend, D. W. Griffiths, as advisor, assistant and actor before being allowed to direct his own films, a series of works that would dissect human foibles with a startling ferocity. His star persona was remarkably strongly delineated and durable but nevertheless not one-dimensional. A series of roles as hateful Prussian and Austrian officers in films shot during the Great War had famously turned him into, as the slogan went, 'the man you love to hate'.[19] In his own films, he had played some very similar characters while adding nuance to his persona. *Blind Husbands* (1919) saw him play the role of an aristocratic Austrian Lieutenant who unscrupulously sets out to seduce a married American woman. In *Foolish Wives* (1921), he is a false count and swindler who seeks to seduce another married American. In *The Wedding March* (1921), he varied the pattern by playing a high-living Austrian prince who, having seen the love of his life killed, joins the army and is killed. Already, at this stage of his career, the principal characteristics of the image were in place. Treacherous villain, heartless seducer or tragic hero, Stroheim is invariably associated with a central European, often aristocratic officer class, even if the association is sometimes fraudulent. He is an archetypal dandy, impeccably dressed, usually in uniform, but always with a hint of vanity, artificiality and excess: white gloves, medals, an ornate sword, more braid than is strictly necessary, and, almost always, a monocle. His bearing reflects the assumed roles: stiffly formal, ramrod stiff back, extravagant heel clicking and, another signature element, the almost always shaven head. The image is at once stereotypical and theatrical in a way that points to the decadent narcissism of a social group and its need to maintain appearances.

Stroheim's image is complicated by his biography, especially by its hidden elements. Having arrived in the USA before the first war, he presented himself as an aristocratic, ex-cavalry officer of the Austro-Hungarian imperial army, a figure very close to the role he would play in many films, very close too to his von Rauffenstein in *La Grande Illusion*. Yet, although he had indeed been a non-commissioned officer in the Austrian army, he had never reached full officer status and had left the army in circumstances that would never be clear. Nor was he an aristocrat. His 'von' was usurped. Stroheim was in fact of middle class Jewish background. While it is routine for actors' private lives to be reworked in the light of their screen persona, Stroheim's case pushes the process to a new level. In a strange game of mirrors within which the boundary between life and performance dissolves, his on-screen persona validates and is validated by the invented persona that he performs in real-life. However, his invented persona is not just any role. It is to some extent a point-by-point negation of the stereotypical Jew. Jews stereotypically have wavy hair. Stroheim has a shaven head. Jews are supposed by anti-Semites to bow and scrape. He is ramrod stiff. He claims to be an officer, a position almost closed to Jews in the Austrian army at the time.[20] His invented persona simultaneously usurps a coveted identity and, in its negative variants, takes revenge on the group to which he had not been allowed to belong. But, of course, none of this was public knowledge until well after his death and it seems almost certain that Renoir was unaware of it. Had he known, the casting of Dalio, the heavily signposted but fully integrated Jew, opposite Stroheim, the hidden one, would have opened up new layers of meaning in the film. The remark by Dalio's character, Rosenthal, that his family has bought up aristocratic castles complete with family portraits has strange echoes of Stroheim's own invention of a noble past.

Stroheim came to France when his American star was very much in decline. His first role there in *Marthe Richard au service de la France* (Bernard, 1937), a clichéd First World War espionage drama, remained absolutely true to type. A ruthless German spy-master, a dandy, a charming seducer, but nonetheless vulnerable, Stroheim reprised familiar elements of his persona. If some of the French roles that he played suggested his image might be broadened to allow him to become another multi-purpose exotic foreigner, his screen appearance and heavily marked performance style ensured that his core characteristics were never dissolved to any great degree. Thus, for example, he played a Chinese warlord in *Les Pirates du rail* but one who, in his bearing and appearance, seemed Prussian through and through! Faced with such a powerful and persistent screen stereotype, Renoir wisely sought to inflect it rather than reinvent it. His Stroheim (von Rauffenstein) is the familiar stereotype of the aristocratic Prussian officer and dandy with swords, braid, medals, shaven head, clicking heels, ramrod back and, of course, the monocle. But von Rauffenstein is purged of any cruelty and given a tragically self-conscious awareness of how his class is condemned by history. The seductiveness of the Stroheim persona is kept – the volume of Casanova's memoirs we see in his castle bedroom is a nod to it – but the main object of the (platonic) seduction is now von Rauffenstein's counterpart, the French aristocratic officer, another theatrical dandy with matching monocle and white gloves. Stroheim's hated 'hun' had once been used to affirm national divisions. Renoir redirects the persona to undermine national boundaries and underscore international class affinities.

Although in almost every way a dissimilar character, Dita Parlo, the German actress, is used to perform a similar task. Parlo had first achieved stardom in the silent era in Germany and briefly sought Hollywood success but France became her main base. She found immediate success there in Jean Vigo's poetic masterpiece, L'Atalante (1934) where she played a sweet, innocent peasant girl, and although she played the same tragic German spy role twice, in G. W. Pabst's Mademoiselle Docteur (1937) and its English remake, her dominant persona probably remained closer to her simple innocence in Vigo's film. Renoir would exploit this quality to the full in La Grande Illusion where Parlo's pure blonde hair served a double role as signifier of innocence and her character's German nationality. Her Elsa is an obvious counterbalance to Stroheim's von Rauffenstein. The simplicity of her surroundings and her modest, peasant costume stand in sharp contrast to the latter's decadent, aristocratic tastes as does Maréchal's simplicity to de Boeldieu's theatrical mannerisms. Her romance with Maréchal opens up the possibility of an internationalism from below to counterbalance the internationalism from above of the career officers.

In La Grande Illusion, Renoir does not use his main performers against type despite a much mythologised reputation for doing so.[21] Rather he picks up the established persona of each star and exploits and reorientates it to fit the needs of a politically progressive narrative, opening Gabin's usually doomed proletarian onto the future, making the mannerisms of Stroheim and the theatrical delivery of Fresnay productive for his story of class and picking up Dalio's often signalled 'foreignness' and using it to undermine ethnically defined visions of nation. Gabin, Dalio, Stroheim and Parlo play a key role in the French cinema of the mid and late 1930s, enacting, across a whole range of films, France's encounter with internal and external others. Stroheim and Parlo would repeatedly play parts in films that explored, in one way or another, the relationship between France and Germany as war approached while Dalio would play a range of exotic parts in the run up to war.[22] Renoir's particularly rich use of them in La Grande Illusion allowed for an examination of Franco-German relations that simultaneously refused any fixed understanding of nation and national belonging.

Renoir would not work again with Parlo or von Stroheim but would with some of the other leading players. He would use them and the echoes they evoked of his earlier works to signal the closing of the window of progressive possibility that the Popular Front had briefly seemed to open. Gabin would again play a proletarian in *La Bête humaine*, but, returning to type, would be unable to escape his past or his tragic fate. Dalio would famously star in *La Règle du jeu*. His Marquis de La Chesnaye in that film might seem a long way from his Rosenthal in *La Grande Illusion*, except that one of La Chesnaye's ancestors happens to be a Rosenthal and the two roles share many traits. The significant difference between Rosenthal and La Chesnaye is that while the former can form a progressive alliance with a proletarian and struggle for liberty, the latter is locked into his own sterile pursuits in a society radically unable to renew itself or face up to threats. Carette's Renoir roles follow a not dissimilar downward trajectory. While he plays a decidedly similar popular character in *La Bête humaine* and *La Règle du jeu*, his loyalty is powerless to save the doomed Gabin in the former while his rebelliousness and frivolity only cause chaos in the latter. The appearances of Stroheim, Parlo and Fresnay in *La Grande Illusion* and of Dalio and Carette in that and other classic Renoir films helped secure their place in the canon of stars and great supporting actors of the period.

War, when it came, would scatter *La Grande Illusion*'s personnel. Renoir made his way to Hollywood. Although his career there was short-lived and not very successful, the United States would remain his main home even after he returned to film-making in Europe. Gabin also left for Hollywood where he made two films. He would return to France as part of the Free French Army, thus converting his fictional soldier of *La Grande Illusion* into a real one. Like Renoir, he would take some time to re-establish himself in the French industry after the conflict. Dalio followed his two compatriots to America, albeit by a very complicated route. He would play exotic characters in a number of Hollywood films when not cast as a stereotypical Frenchman, as in Michael Curtiz's *Casablanca* (1942) where he played a croupier. While in exile he would discover that his image had been used to represent the 'typical' Jew in anti-Semitic propaganda in Paris. Tragically, he would later learn that his mother, father and sisters had been killed in the

Nazi death camps.[23] Stroheim also wisely returned to his adopted homeland for the duration of the war, a period when German officer roles were in good supply. Other characters stayed behind in France, where, after an initial period of disruption, the French industry thrived, partly because both the occupier and the collaborationist Vichy regime were keen to keep it active, partly because Hollywood films were soon banned from French screens. Fresnay would star in one of the outstanding films of the period, Henry-Georges Clouzot's *Le Corbeau* (1943), a work whose scathing portrayal of French provincial society would cause problems for director and star at the Liberation, also an uneasy time for *La Grande Illusion*.

Historical and political contexts

La Grande Illusion is a film about the Great War or First World War made during the period of the French Popular Front. It thus requires a double historical contextualisation that discusses both the war and the Popular Front. It might indeed be more accurate to say that it requires us to look at how the war was seen at the time of the Front, especially by those like Renoir who were so clearly affiliated to the political left.

There is still no single or consensual way to see the war.[24] One productive way to approach it might be to see it as a watershed between the nineteenth and twentieth centuries, the end of a century of *relative* internal European peace (from 1815 to 1914) and the beginning of the barbarity of the short twentieth century (two world wars, genocide, the Gulag). The Europe that began the war was one that could still hold onto romantic visions of conflict, of acts of individual courage or of collective heroism. But, once it was under way, such visions seemed condemned by the mass, anonymous slaughter of trench warfare and by the fact that it was clearly the ability to mobilise entire countries and their productive capacity that would determine the outcome. An increasingly educated and technologically sophisticated Europe might have seemed to be becoming ever more advanced, ever more civilised. But when education had served to inculcate nationalism in the masses rather than free them, and technology had been put in the service of slaughter, belief in progress or civilisation were hard to maintain. The war could indeed be seen to have brutalised the European masses, teaching them to hold life cheaply and persuading them of the value of discipline in a way that prepared for the bitterness of twentieth century social struggles and for genocide.[25]

If the war was difficult for any group to digest, it posed particular problems for the left. It had been hoped by socialists that a European conflict could be prevented by mass strike action by the working classes of the different countries involved. But the strikes did not happen and rather than opposing the war, leftist parties and trade unions became sucked into its planning and organisation. In France, the Socialist leader Jaurès, the great spokesman of pacifism, was assassinated on the eve of the conflict. At his funeral, the General Secretary of the CGT, the trade union confederation, famously declared, 'we will be the soldiers of liberty', thus signalling the abandonment of opposition to war and renunciation of the planned use of the general strike to prevent mobilisation.[26] The war exposed the weakness of socialist internationalism. The 'Internationale', might have seemed to have displaced the 'Marseillaise' as song of the workers since its composition in 1888, but the war quickly saw the revenge of the latter. French revolutionary mythology was all too easily mobilised to legitimise the conflict. If France, the land of liberty and equality, had been attacked by a militaristic Germany, then the citizen-soldiers going to her defence could be presented as the heirs of those had gone to the frontier to defend a fledgling revolution from invasion. The 'Marseillaise' had started life, one should remember, as the battle hymn of the French army of the Rhine and it is no accident that the body of its composer, Rouget de Lisle, was dug up and transferred to the Invalides, with due pomp and ceremony on 14 July 1915 as part of the propagandist mise-en-scène surrounding the war.[27] When the song is heard in *La Grande Illusion*, we should clearly bear this wartime use in mind.

In the aftermath of the war, the left had somehow to deal with its failure to mount meaningful opposition to it. One way to make sense of what had happened, to be born in mind when we consider the politics of *La Grande Illusion*, was to interpret the war as the last gasp of the old European order. The post-war disappearance of the old, hereditary ruling classes could be seen to clear the way for the necessary showdown between workers and capitalists. The war could also be incorporated into a vision of historical progress if it was seen as paving the way for Revolution, as it had in Russia. But the Russian revolution could not explain away the seduction of the French left by nationalism and the apparent compliance of the working class in mass slaughter.[28] Perhaps, indeed, the failings of the left had their roots in the revolutionary tradition itself. Had the French Revolution not fallen prey to nationalist aggression and, by militarising itself, paved the way for Bonapartist dictatorship and the subordination of popular rule to the men in uniform?[29]

In the early 1930s, Europe might have seemed to be on the road to peace, with leading politicians on both sides of the Rhine seeming committed to moving in that direction. But hopes soon dimmed. 1933 saw the Nazis come to power in Germany and the reappearance of German militarism. With Italy also under fascist rule, democracy was increasingly threatened across the continent. Nor was France itself free of fear of fascism, as was underlined, in February 1934, when a right-wing march in Paris sought to attack the parliament in what was seen by some as an attempted coup. The French left united in the face of the fascist menace, now seen as the main threat. The Communists, the Socialists and the Radical party came together to form the Popular Front. The Front won the 1936 elections, a result which famously triggered a wave of strikes and factory occupations, which in turn produced significant gains for the working class. But stormy waters lay ahead. The Front was an unstable coalition and was in trouble by 1937, not least because of foreign policy divisions.

1936 saw the outbreak of civil war in Spain and, while Germany and Italy freely intervened in support of Franco's military coup, Britain and France failed to move in support of the democratically elected Spanish government. While the Communists pressed for involvement, the Socialists reluctantly held back. Divided on Spain, the French left was also deeply split on how to respond to the increasingly obvious threat from Nazi militarism and fascism more generally. On the one hand, there were the integral pacifists who felt that France had to avoid a conflict at all costs. On the other hand, there were those, notably the Communists, who were driven primarily by antifascism and who, although they too would claim the pacifist label, maintained that it was vital to mobilise in the face of the threat. While the singing of the 'Marseillaise' had once seemed completely discredited due to its wartime mobilisation, elements of the left including the Communists, readopted it at the time of the Popular Front. Nationalism, once a dirty word, regained respectability as the Front sought to reclaim symbols of nation from the right as part of its attempt to occupy the middle ground of

French politics and block the path of any indigenous fascism. At the same time, the rehabilitation of French revolutionary nationalism and its symbols was a way to remind the French of the need to be prepared to defend the French Republic against foreign threat.[30]

The struggle over the definition of the nation also inevitably revolved around who could and should be admitted into it. Reconstruction after the Great War and the return of economic growth had stimulated a massive wave of immigration. With the worldwide economic depression of the 1930s and the rise of unemployment it brought with it, racism almost inevitably followed.[31] The far right was clearly able to feed off and stoke the xenophobic outpouring, but no sector of French opinion could automatically be assumed to be immune from it. Racism and anti-Semitism were not simply to be found on the other side of the Rhine. France had its own indigenous traditions going back to the nineteenth century and coming to a previous peak around the time of the celebrated Dreyfus affair, during Renoir's childhood. The 1930s brought this ugly tradition back to the surface with a vengeance. If the danger of the French revolutionary inheritance was its capacity to mutate into military expansionism and dictatorial tyranny, the darkest side of French nationalism was the racist tradition that was part of it.

Arising out of the context of the Popular Front, Renoir's cinema of that period is at least partially a response to and intervention in debates and struggles around the nation and its traditions.[32] More specifically, *La Grande Illusion* is an attempt to make productive sense of the First World War within the French republican and revolutionary traditions while at the same time responding to the challenges of the 1930s. This is a difficult challenge that the film would meet in a range of ways. For example, the important role it gives to its Jewish character is clearly a response to the xenophobia and anti-Semitism that so marked the 1930s. Yet it could not wear its anti-Fascism on its sleeve without becoming anachronistic. Similarly, if it was to reflect the First World War accurately without undermining its own Frontist politics, it would need to bear witness to the aggressive nationalist upsurge that so characterised the wartime period while maintaining a critical distance from it. Caught between two contexts, it would need to deal with one (the war) explicitly and the other (the 1930s) implicitly. This inevitably condemned it to an ambiguity that would contribute to its overwhelming success in 1937 but which would come back to haunt it when it was re-released after the Second World War.

Notes

1   Bergan, *Jean Renoir*, pp. 41–49.
2   Renoir, Jean, *Ma Vie et mes films* (Paris, 1974), p. 145.
3   One might find echoes of *Tire-au-flanc*'s barrack room comedy in the depiction of the first prison camp in *La Grande Illusion*. A concert complete with comic cross-dressing in the earlier film also prefigures the famous concert scene of its celebrated successor. At the level of detail, the famous scene in *La Grande Illusion* where von Rauffenstein cuts the only flower of the prison fortress that he presides over in honour of his dead French prisoner is prefigured, in *Tire-au-flanc*, when an officer plucks a solitary rose growing by the hero's prison cell window.
4   O'Shaughnessy, Martin, *Jean Renoir* (Manchester, 2000), pp. 86–91.
5   Bazin, André, *Jean Renoir* (Paris, 1989), pp. 40–43.
6   Bazin, *Jean Renoir*, pp. 79–84.
7   Faulkner, *The Social Cinema of Jean Renoir*, pp. 49–50, 61.
8   Renoir's columns for *Ce Soir* are gathered together in Renoir, Jean, *Ecrits 1926–1971* (Paris: 1974), pp. 96–183 (edited by Claude Gauteur).
9   Ory, Pascal, *La belle illusion: culture et politique sous le signe du Front Populaire, 1935-1938* (Paris, 1994), pp. 439–444.
10 Ibid., p. 450.
11 O'Shaughnessy, Martin, 'La Règle du jeu', in P. Powrie (ed.), *The Cinema of France* (London, 2004), pp. 40–49.
12 O'Shaughnessy, *Jean Renoir*, pp. 120-123.
13 Crisp, Colin, *The Classic French Cinema, 1930-1960* (Bloomington, Indiana, 1997).
14 Vincendeau, Ginette, *Stars and Stardom in French Cinema* (London, 2000), p. 61.
15 Ibid., pp. 72–73.
16 Ibid., pp. 70–73.
17 Ibid., pp. 61, 71–72.
18 Ibid., pp. 68–69.
19 Quinn Curtiss, Thomas, *Von Stroheim* (New York, 1971), pp. 79–92.
20 Lignon, Fanny, *Erich von Stroheim: du ghetto au Gotha* (Paris, 1998), pp. 12–27, 319.
21 Renoir's reputation as someone who habitually sought to give his productions spontaneous life by casting against type and improvising on set is dissected by Curchod who reminds us that the director generally preferred to follow the script in a disciplined manner and had no systematic policy of casting against type even if the development of roles and the contingencies of production sometimes made that appear to be the case. See Curchod, Olivier, 'La "Méthode Renoir" et ses légendes: petite histoire d'un casting "provocateur"', *Genesis 28* (2007), pp. 73–88.
22 Apart from the two versions of *Mademoiselle Docteur* mentioned earlier, Parlo was in Choux's *Ultimatum* (1938) and *Paix sur le Rhin* (1938). Stroheim was also in the second version of *Mademoiselle Docteur* and *Ultimatum*. He appeared minus Parlo in Gréville's *Menaces*, a film about the approaching conflict. Apart from Dalio's lead roles in *La Règle du jeu* and Chenal's already mentioned *La*

Maison du Maltais, his role as sultan in Sorkin's *L'Esclave blanche* (1939) gives some sense of what he was asked to do.

23 Dalio, Marcel, *Mes années folles* (Paris, 1976), pp. 146–147, 215–217.

24 See Prost, Antoine and Winter, Jay, *Penser la Grande Guerre: un essai d'historiographie* (Paris, 2004).

25 Mosse, George, *Fallen Soldiers: Reshaping the Memory of the World Wars* (Oxford, 1990), pp. 160–175.

26 Prost and Winter, *Penser la Grande Guerre*, p. 176.

27 Ben-Amos, Avner, 'The "Marseillaise" as myth and metaphor: the transfer of Rouget de Lisle to the Invalides during the Great War', in V. Holman and D. Kelly, *France at War in the Twentieth Century: Propaganda, Myth and Metaphor* (Oxford, 2000), pp. 42-46.

28 A still hotly contested issue is the extent to which common Frenchmen were willing participants in the war or were effectively compelled to fight. See Prost and Winter, *Penser la Grande Guerre*, pp. 140–143.

29 Luzzatto, Sergio, *L'Impôt du sang: la gauche française à l'épreuve de la guerre mondiale 1900–1945* (Lyon, 1996), pp. 99–100, 110.

30 Luzzatto, *L'Impot du sang*, pp. 105–128.

31 Noiriel, Gérard, *Le Creuset français. Histoire de l'immigration, XIXe–XXe siècles* (Paris, 1988), pp. 247–294.

32 O'Shaughnessy, *Jean Renoir*, pp. 123–140.

2 Genesis, evolution, preparation

A long gestation

The gestation period of *La Grande Illusion* was about two and a half years. Renoir recalls that the initial idea for the film first came to him when he was filming *Toni* on location in the south of France in the Autumn of 1934. Attracted by the presence of a film crew, airmen from a local base were flying low over the shooting and interfering with the work. When Renoir contacted the base, he discovered an old acquaintance, First World War fighter ace Pinsard, a man who had rescued Renoir's slow-flying reconnaissance aircraft from enemy attack. The ever sociable Renoir took to dining with Pinsard after shooting and the latter told him about his multiple escapes from German prisoner-of-war camps during the war.[1] Sometime afterwards, probably early in 1935, Renoir produced a film outline based on Pinsard's stories called *Les Evasions du Colonel Pinsard*.[2] Never previously analysed, as far as I can ascertain, this initial outline will be discussed shortly. The next important step in the film's genesis was when Renoir invited Charles Spaak to help him develop the script. By Spaak's account they had already begun to work on *La Grande Illusion* before they collaborated on *Les Bas-fonds*. A first treatment was produced. According to Spaak, this drew on the experience of his older brother, Paul-Henri, who had been captured and imprisoned while fighting for Belgium in the war, as well as on Renoir's memories of his time as a reconnaissance pilot. He and Renoir also interviewed representatives of escaped prisoners' organisations, but drew very little on their accounts.[3] They consulted other sources, notably prisoner-of-war memoirs and stories, although it is hard to pin influences down precisely. One that does stand out is the novel *Kavalier Scharnhorst* by Jean des Vallières, which became, as we shall see, the subject of a famous plagiarism case brought against the film.

Renoir and Spaak found it impossible to interest any producers in their initial treatment of the film. However, having been engaged by the producer Kamenka to work on *Les Bas-fonds*, the pair offered *La Grande Illusion* to him. Kamenka was happy to back the project but could not find the financial collaborators that he needed. A budget was nonetheless drawn up with projected costs – about 1.5m francs – that were no more than the average costs for a major film in the French cinema of the time.[4] Crucially too, Jean Gabin, the star of *Les Bas-fonds*, became a strong believer in the project. Gabin's enthusiasm was a key factor in Renoir's eventual ability to gain backing from the recently established Société des Réalisations d'Art Cinématographique (RAC), run by the financier Frank Rollmer, assisted by Albert Pinkevitch. The contract with RAC was signed on 9 November 1936. At this stage the cast was to include Gabin, Jouvet (as de Boeldieu), Pierre Renoir (as a German camp commander), and Robert le Vigan (as Gabin's initial partner in the escape). What is striking is how close this cast – especially the Gabin-Jouvet pairing – is to that of *Les Bas-fonds*. The resemblance is even more striking if one remembers that the class locations of the pair as proletarian and aristocrat were to remain the same. Signature of the contract meant work could begin in earnest. In the meantime, the script was developing. A second draft, a dialogue script in Spaak's handwriting, was produced, probably in the Autumn of 1936.[5] The third draft bears the date (in Spaak's handwriting) of November–December 1936 and is a type-written shooting script, complete with dialogue, camera shots and locations.[6]

In November 1936 Renoir left for Alsace to scout out locations with key members of the production team, including Spaak, Christian Matras, the cinematographer, Jacques Becker his assistant, Carl Koch, his assistant/advisor, Eugène Lourié, the set designer, and Rollmer and Pinkevitch, the producers. The two principal locations sought were the two prisoner-of-war camps. According to Lourié's memoirs, the first to be found was the Haut-Koenigsbourg castle which would become the Wintersborn camp in the film. A forbidding mediaeval structure perched on a commanding height, it had been substantially rebuilt at the beginning of the twentieth century by Kaiser Wilhelm at a time when the disputed provinces, Alsace and Lorraine, were under German control.[7] Given the impossibility of shooting in Nazi dominated Germany, Alsace was the ideal stand-in location due to the strong Germanic influence on its architectural styles. It would also have been a constant reminder to the crew and cast of the ongoing Franco-German military rivalry as it had changed hands after the Prussian victory over France in 1870 only to revert back to France in 1918. Location scouting continued as the group looked for an isolated mountain farmhouse and found an ideal one, by a country road, overlooking a valley.[8] This would be Elsa's farm in the finished film. Their final port of call would be the historic garrison town of Colmar, a town whose barracks would play the role of the Hallbach camp in the film.

The casting of the film was far from incident free and changes were to have an enormous impact on the final work. If the unavailable Jouvet's replacement with Fresnay did not cause major changes to the script, the hiring of Dita Parlo would have a significant impact. Then, in January, just before shooting was due to start, Erich von Stroheim was brought into the cast by the production director who hired him for a small part, reportedly without realising the fame of the person he was dealing with.[9] To cater for the presence of a cinematic legend whose films he had himself revered, Renoir was forced to undertake a major last-minute rewrite of his film, abetted by Koch, Becker and, to a very limited extent, Spaak. The arrival of Stroheim can easily overshadow another momentous change. In the second part of the film in all the drafts, Gabin's Maréchal was to escape with a character called Dolette, an intellectual. Robert le Vigan, who had played in *Les Bas-fonds*, was originally wanted for this part but turned it down. It would be Rosenthal, the Jewish character played by Dalio who would escape with Maréchal, his role thus taking on much greater significance than originally intended. Le Vigan's refusal was a great blessing in disguise. Another of French cinema's strong supporting actors, he tended to play troubled characters and visionaries, no doubt because of the intensity of his screen presence and his rather ascetic features. An alcoholic actor in Renoir's *Les Bas-fonds*, he plays Christ in Duvivier's *Golgotha*. He was also a friend of the great writer and notorious anti-Semite Louis Ferdinand Céline. After 1940 and the fall of France, he became drawn into Parisian collaborationist circles and made anti-Semitic radio broadcasts for Radio Paris. He was unsurprisingly convicted and sentenced at the Liberation, his French acting career at an end. His presence in *La Grande Illusion* would undoubtedly have affected how people later saw the film, especially given its problematic post-war reception.

After the exteriors had been scouted and necessary measurements taken, Lourié was able to design and build the matching interiors on the sound stages of the Tobis and Éclair studios in Epinay. Shooting was to be split between two studios because insufficient space was available at the film's main base at Tobis.[10] However, it was the exteriors that would be shot first, during the whole month of February, with the cold and difficult conditions that one would expect. Interior shooting began on 1 March and went on into April with shooting taking place in plot order. The final shots, the escape over the border into Switzerland, were shot in the French Alps at Chamonix, but without the presence of Gabin who was working on another film by then. A double would take his place.[11] Promotion for the film began at the end of April in the trade press and continued in the mainstream press from the end of May in the lead up to the première on the 8th June at the Marivaux cinema in Paris.[12]

The evolving script

Study of the genesis of *La Grande Illusion* has relied up to now on the three known drafts of the film, the Spaak signed outline published in Bazin's *Renoir* and the dialogue and shooting scripts held in the BIFI archives. Renoir's own plot outline, *Les Evasions du Colonel Pinsard*, can now cast further light on the project's evolution. It represents a fascinating 'missing link' between the film's initial inspiration and the known versions of the script. If it is still close in some ways to published versions of Pinsard's adventures, it also clearly attempts to build a fiction from his story.

As we know, the initial idea for *La Grande Illusion* sprang from a series of meetings between Renoir and ace flyer and escapee Pinsard. Accounts of Pinsard's escapes were on public record as early as 1917 in successive numbers of *La Vie aérienne illustrée*, an illustrated magazine of the time that played a major part in taking tales of aviation heroism to a public in search of heroes. Reading the pages it devotes to Pinsard, one can already recognize what were to become elements of the film: Pinsard's reconnaissance mission with an observer whose name (Amaudric de Chauffaud) suggests aristocratic origins; a forced landing behind enemy lines followed by imprisonment; repeated failed attempts to escape; a period of solitary confinement (35 days) in an airless, unlit cell; a kindly gaoler who saves Pinsard from despair; the tears of Pinsard's comrades when he is helped back to his cell, unable to walk unaided; the final escape with Ménard (another flyer); Ménard's damaged foot; passage into Switzerland. A more developed account of Pinsard and Ménard's escape from the late 1920s adds some details that the film would also make use of: after being shot down, Pinsard is driven to the local German headquarters for interrogation and then invited to dinner by the colonel; a tunnel is dug in one camp with the digger maintaining contact with his comrades by means of a cord tied to his leg; the escape fails when the men are transferred to another camp on the eve of the break-out.[13] Interestingly too, Pinsard's rank at the start of the war, 'Maréchal des logis', offers one obvious source for the name of the hero of Renoir's film. It is of course impossible to know what further details Pinsard transmitted orally to Renoir. But what is clear is that at least some key elements of Pinsard's story found their way into the finished film.

Les Evasions du Colonel Pinsard, the outline that Renoir developed from Pinsard's accounts is clearly already semi-fictional. We can tell this not least because Renoir's Pinsard escapes with 'X', the observer with whom he had been shot down, while the real Pinsard escapes with Ménard, another flyer. Renoir's version also makes Pinsard's escape coincide with the French recapture of the fort of Douaumont and the singing of the 'Marseillaise', nationalist high-spots that would surely have been included in earlier published accounts if they were true. Finally, Renoir's fictionalisation contains a rather improbable tale of romance, jealousy and betrayal that suggests an attempt to inject drama and emotion into the story rather than a respect for historical accuracy. The main interest of Renoir's Pinsard outline lies less, however, in how it respects or betrays Pinsard's story and more in how it moves us towards the film that would finally emerge. I present it in the table in Appendix three, alongside the first draft proper of the film, changes made by the second and third drafts, and the film itself, all in summary form.

Close examination of the project's evolution shows that it changes in a series of ways, some more and some less predictable, as it moves from the initial Pinsard outline, through the different drafts, to the completed work. Predictably, for example, more and more details are filled in as the film approaches its completed form: indications of the songs that will be heard start to appear by the second and third drafts of the film proper; supporting roles are delineated with more precision (by being given names and social statuses); dialogue is added with much of it present in near definitive form by the time of the final draft of the script despite some important changes still to come. Other, less predictable changes are worth discussing in more detail.

One might begin with the shifting place and weight of some of the film's core themes. Social class is a good place to start. Although implicitly present in the initial Pinsard outline (the German officers dining in the captured château, the simple generosity of the German guard when Pinsard is in solitary), it is relatively unaccented not least because no clear indication is given of the central character's class identity. By the first draft proper, class has become the central theme. The hero, now named Maréchal, is given a clearly proletarian identity that allows the sharp contrast with the aristocratic de Boeldieu to take shape. Dolette's identification as an intellectual adds the educated middle class to the mix. The first draft proper's pessimistic ending – the failure of Maréchal and Dolette to rendez-vous in Maxim's – suggests that the coming together of proletarian and intellectual permitted by the war will not survive the peace, the 'grande illusion' of the film's title thereby perhaps being that class reconciliation could continue beyond the conflict.[14] If we accept this reading, then subsequent drafts might seem to blur the vision of sharp class distinctions by developing the themes of nationalism, internationalism and anti-Semitism and allowing the question of the separation or continued friendship of Rosenthal and Maréchal to remain open in the film itself. On the other hand, there is a progressive clarification of the class dimension of the sacrifice that allows for the escape. Mobilising a range of characters in the Pinsard outline, the sacrifice still includes a cheeky Parisian alongside de Boeldieu in the first draft proper.[15] Narrowing itself down to de Boeldieu in the final drafts, it reaches its highest level of class-consciousness in the film itself.

On the question of internationalism, it is interesting to note that the Pinsard outline is in some ways more international than the first draft proper, essentially because Pinsard's companions in the first camp embrace four different nationalities while Maréchal's room-mates from the first draft onwards are purely French. But the international nature of the outline's characters should not lead us to assume that it is internationalist in spirit. Although it already contains the early Franco-German dinner and the kindly German guard, it is still distinctly nationalist in tone. The final, successful escape is associated with the French recapture of the key fort of Douaumont and the singing of a jubilant 'Marseillaise', while the proposed epilogue, with its celebration of the exploits and skills of a French air ace seems close to nationalist hagiography. When the 'Marseillaise' and Douaumont are relocated in later drafts, the film simultaneously purges the escape of nationalism and allows for a self-reflexive examination of its seduction during the entertainment sequence. At the same time, we see the progressive rebuilding of an international *and* internationalist dimension as the project evolves. Russian prisoners are reintroduced, the presence of the English increased, notably in the entertainment sequences, and the relationships between Maréchal and Elsa and von Rauffenstein and de Boeldieu developed. Elsa's initially minor role has become a major one by the time of the later drafts.

Showing even more startling growth, von Rauffenstein only emerges as a major character in the film itself, clearly due to the casting of von Stroheim and the need to give him a role commensurate with his reputation. The character emerges with the fusion of two parts (the senior German officer who entertains the flyers and the prison camp commander). Yet much of his growth occurs because existing episodes are altered to give him a more central role (unlike in any of the drafts, for example, he himself will shoot de Boeldieu) and new episodes are added (the tour of the castle, the tête-à-tête with de Boeldieu, the deathbed scene). The role's dramatic expansion makes the film's examination of class considerably more international while at the same time giving the aristocracy a much greater place than in the drafts. This would push some to see the film as an elegiac celebration of a declining ruling class and therefore to question its progressive credentials.

The theme of anti-Semitism is absent from the initial Pinsard outline and the first draft proper, only being introduced in the second and third drafts of the script. Even then, it is relatively undeveloped, not least because the Jewish character's presence is limited to the first prison camp. It is only in the film itself that Rosenthal grows to absorb Dolette, allowing the Maréchal-Rosenthal pairing to balance the de Boeldieu-von Rauffenstein couple and Jewishness and anti-Semitism to become central themes. It is interesting, while on this subject, to note the evolution of the relationship between the two escapees. The question over whether the hero will go on without his injured friend runs through all the different versions but only in the initial Pinsard outline and in the film itself does a character's injury and slowness cause a quarrel. In the outline, the ostensible pretext is the stench of Ménard's injured foot. In the film itself the injury is overlain with Rosenthal's Jewishness. The resurrection of an abandoned plot sub-element to engage with anti-Semitism underscores how the film's plot is progressively inhabited – put to work – by its politics.

Gender is not explicitly present as a theme in the Pinsard outline which does however establish, in a sketchy way, a polarised representation of women when a woman worker falls for Pinsard while another woman, a secretary, observes and informs upon men preparing an escape. This polarisation is more pronounced in the first draft proper through the contrasting figures of the sadistic temptress who seeks to humiliate the prisoners and the German peasant woman who sleeps with both escapees. Present in the three drafts of the film proper, the temptress infuses the emergent film with a regressive sexual politics by allowing a female scapegoat to be punished for the male unmanning associated with captivity. The other woman provides some balance by suggesting how a German woman and a Frenchman can come together harmoniously when freed from relationships of domination and subordination. This sexual encounter lays the ground for the decidedly more romantic Franco-German rapprochement of Maréchal and Elsa that would displace it from draft two onwards. The sexually available peasant woman should not however be seen as a purely positive figure. Her brief encounter with the two men would seem to serve more to underscore their bonding – their capacity to share *everything* – than it does to open up space for the exploration of women's experience of war. If the more substantial character of Elsa was to help correct this neglect, it would be above all the theatrical entertainment (present from the first draft on), with its scenes of cross-dressing, that would open the way for an exploration and destabilisation of gender identities and move the film well beyond the rather conventional gender roles of the Pinsard outline.

In contrast to these sharp thematic shifts, the film's apparently unchanging generic identity as war film and escape drama might suggest an area of stability. Yet closer examination reveals that it also evolves considerably in this respect. The war film is inevitably associated with scenes of combat and action. While the prisoner-of-war sub-genre might lessen the expectation of such scenes, it is significant that the drafts of the film suggest a greater role for visible action than in the finished film. For example, the first draft proper suggests shots including the following: the plane taking off; views from the cockpit; the plane as it loses height; German soldiers on the ground; the flyers setting light to the plane on the ground. The final draft, the shooting script, likewise anticipated having shots of the airfield, aerial shots, shots of soldiers in the trenches looking up, of German fighters and a dogfight in which a German plane would be shot down. None of this action would be seen in the film. Its continuing story role would be indicated by the ellipsis between the two Frenchmen preparing to leave the French mess and von Rauffenstein announcing his 'kill'. The dogfight and death of a pilot from the shooting script would translate into the distinctly unspectacular presence of a wreath in the film itself. A similar reduction of visible action would characterise the end of the film. The Pinsard outline foresaw exchange of gunfire between the French prisoners and their guards. The first draft proper also anticipated an exchange of shots, with de Boeldieu and the Parisian escaping to the roof with a revolver. By the time of the finished film, de Boeldieu would be armed only with a flute! The drafts indicated a degree of action surrounding the escape with successive versions mentioning the escapees being sought in a forest by men with lights (the first draft proper) and pursuit by dogs, with the men having to hide under sticks (drafts two and three). In the film itself, pursuit is only implied by barked order from von Rauffenstein. The broad pattern behind these changes is a progressive shift of emphasis from sequences to scenes, from action to interaction and from spectacle to dialogue.

The finished film would also be less brutal than the drafts, not simply because the spectacle of combat would be largely absent from it, but also because the interaction of the characters would be softened in a range of ways.[16] In the Pinsard outline and in the first draft proper, for example, the two downed airmen are beaten by troops on the ground for trying to set light to their aircraft. In the film itself, this beating has disappeared.

Similarly, there is an indication in the first draft that German guards intervene violently to subdue the Frenchmen singing the 'Marseillaise'. In the film itself, this violence is not shown. The first three drafts all contain, of course, the misogynistic story of the sadistic temptress and her punishment, a story shed from the film. The Pinsard story has the two escapees cross the border while a guard is distracted. The first draft has the two men kill the guard, a violent act that again disappears from the completed work. As we have noted, the First World War is often seen as the event that began the twentieth century's brutalisation of international relations and internal politics. Rather perversely perhaps, going against the grain, Renoir's film project seems characterised by a progressive de-brutalisation that opens up space for its burgeoning internationalism.

What factors brought about the changes we have identified? While it is probably impossible to tie factors to changes with absolute precision, we can suggest with reasonable confidence that the following came into play:

1 Pragmatic concerns of time and money:

   The obvious case where money came into play is in the replacement of the planned château sequence with the simple flyers' hut that we see in the film itself, apparently because the producers took fright at the potential cost involved.[17] The removal of the château meant that the German staff officers associated with it were shed from the film. We might suggest more tentatively that the abandonment of planned shots of aerial dogfights and ground action was to do with the cost of such filming and the time it would take. Thus, while it might be tempting to see the predominance of group interaction over action in the finished film as a direct consequence of Renoir's directorial preferences, one should also consider that Renoir, as an ex-flyer, might have liked to include shots of aerial action but was deterred from doing so by practical issues.

2 The input of Spaak:

   Because Spaak worked closely with Renoir, it is impossible to separate out their two inputs with precision. It is nonetheless striking that the first draft proper – the moment when Spaak's influence initially came into play – shows a very distinct sharpening of the project's dramatic structure. The initial Pinsard outline had three main escape attempts, two in the first camp and one in the second. The first draft proper has one escape attempt in each camp, providing for a more balanced structure. In the same draft, the film's class oppositions are etched in with sharp contours as characters begin to acquire specific identities. At this stage too, as we have seen, the story is a very hard-edged one, with more brutality than the finished work and a grimmer ending. Given that Spaak's input was largely over after the writing of the shooting script, it is tempting to attribute the final 'softening' of the film to Renoir.

3 Changes to the cast:
The casting of Dita Parlo, which almost certainly took place between the first and second drafts of the film, is the obvious explanation for the growth of the role of Elsa. Similarly the casting of von Stroheim explains the dramatic growth of his role. The importance acquired by von Rauffenstein may also help explain the parallel growth in the role of Rosenthal, an evolution that allowed the democratic Rosenthal-Maréchal axis to provide a necessary counterweight to the aristocrats. But the withdrawal of Le Vigan from the project and the need to reallocate his part was clearly also a factor. *La Grande Illusion*'s multilingualism is so famous that we now tend to assume that it was hard-wired into the project from the start. However, while it was indeed part of the film from an early stage, being explicitly mentioned in the first draft proper, its final extent is undoubtedly contingent upon the film's casting. Had von Stroheim not been hired, had both he and Fresnay not been able to speak English and had Dalio not been a confident German speaker, there would have been considerably less space for multilingualism in the finished work.

4 Contextual factors:
The film was drafted and redrafted at the time of the Popular Front and in the face of the internal and international fascist threat by a politically committed director and a script-writer with avowed leftist leanings. The Pinsard outline seems bereft of a politics. If anything, it comes close to nationalist hagiography. This is not a little surprising given that it comes from broadly the same period as *Toni,* a film that suggested emergent politicisation due to its proletarian hero and its refusal of an exclusionary vision of nation. What is far less surprising is that subsequent drafts of

the film and the film itself are clearly inhabited by the politics of the day, with anti-fascism, internationalism, class opposition and a sense of history all shaping the emerging work.

La Grande Illusion is such a beautifully crafted film that it is easy to think that it was always destined to take the shape that it finally did. Analysis of its genesis suggests that its final form was in fact contingent on a range of factors and that, given changes in any of these, it could have shifted in different directions. The picture of the project's evolution becomes even more complex when we put what we know of the shooting process back into the picture and particularly when we remind ourselves that the film as it was finally shot depended on what the director, actors and technicians did with the script in the sets that were built and the locations chosen. We will discuss the set after looking at the plagiarism allegations.

The plagiarism case

If Pinsard's story was an unproblematic and openly acknowledged source for *La Grande Illusion*, another source, Jean des Vallières' *Kavalier Scharnhorst*, was decidedly more controversial, given that its author was to take out a lawsuit for partial plagiarism against Spaak and Renoir after the film's release.[18] A letter Renoir sends to des Vallières and his publishers in June 1937 seeks to provide a point-by-point refutation of the plagiarism allegations, citing a wide range of sources for all that is contained in the film (personal acquaintances, written memoirs, the League of Wartime Escapees, documentation gathered by Koch, Renoir's German adviser, and so on).[19] Renoir's vigorous defence was a little disingenuous, given that it seems clear that he and/or Spaak had indeed read and used elements of des Vallières' book. Some of the most telling examples are as follows:

1   *Kavalier Scharnhorst* begins with a flyer being shot down and captured. On the ground he meets a German aviator who speaks fluent French because he has worked for five years as a mechanic at the Blériot works. The film picks this up almost exactly, except that the German has worked at the Gnôme works.

2   There is a Frenchman in the book whose party piece is to sing 'Il était un petit navire', the song heard twice in Renoir's film although put to very different use.

3   A German officer at one camp in the book has a mistress who likes to taunt the French prisoners by parading partially or completely naked in full view of them. This woman would seem a very likely source for the sadistic temptress who traversed three drafts of the film.

4   English prisoners in one camp in the book put on a theatrical show involving cross-dressing. English prisoners similarly cross-dress in Renoir's film.

5   The book suggests that the word *Verboten* is the key to German civilian and military education. The film uses *Verboten* as a leitmotiv.

6   One prisoner in the book is translating Horace, a classical poet. In the film, it is Pindar, another classical poet.

7   The prisoners in the book's final camp create an enormous amount of noise to express their refusal to submit to German authority. Prisoners in the film create a din to cover the escape.

These different points suggest that the book clearly did influence the film at an early stage with convergences occurring from the first draft proper onwards in a way that suggests that Spaak drew on des Vallières' text to add colour to Renoir's initial Pinsard draft. However, the influence seems relatively trivial, involving only minor characters or relatively unimportant details. Other convergences between film and book might build a case for more serious plagiarism: the book's captured airman is invited to dine with chivalrous German flyers; it talks of characters who struggle to complete a tunnel due to suffocation; having started out in prison camps that seem like holiday camps, the book's hero is sent to a fortress prison with a rigorous regime along with other recalcitrant prisoners. But some of these convergences, like the dinner invitation, or the austere final camp can equally be traced back to Pinsard's source story. In the end, it is unsurprising that des Vallières failed to make his case stick.

At one stage it seemed that des Vallières' case was not only about plagiarism. A letter Renoir wrote to Aragon, the editor of the Communist paper *Ce Soir*, suggests he feared that the accusation would be used by the extreme right-wing press to discredit a known leftist intellectual while furthering its struggle with the Popular Front over definitions of the nation. He wrote:

> His [des Vallières'] friends from *Candide, Gringoire, L'Action française* [extreme-rightist publications], are only too happy to support him in his attempt to prove that an author classified as left-wing can't produce a national subject without stealing it from them ... It's a question of insinuating that all which is national ... belongs exclusively to the fascists.[20]

The set

It would undoubtedly be an exaggeration to claim that Renoir's mature style of the later 1930s could not have emerged without Lourié, not least because it was not him but Jean Castanier who designed the set for *Le Crime de Monsieur Lange*, one of the films where the style finds its most flamboyant expression. What is clear however is that Lourié's designs were essential not only to the look of some of Renoir's great works, but also to how they were filmed and how their images were composed. The influence of set designer on director is not a one-way process. Lourié knew how Renoir liked to film and built his sets accordingly. But once the sets were complete, they opened up new filming possibilities.[21] While it would be wrong to see Renoir as a happy on-set improviser, definitive camera movements and positions were only worked out once rehearsals were able to move into the completed set. Lourié describes the process thus:

> Rehearsing with actors, Renoir would sit them around the table on the set, running over their dialogue ... little by little, the relationship between characters developed, their personalities sharpened, and the scene took shape. New dialogue was sketched in and logical stage movements were suggested by Renoir. Usually Christian Matras, the lighting cameraman (or director of photography), and Claude Renoir, Jean's nephew and the camera operator, were present at rehearsals and with Jean they decided on the mechanics of shooting the sequence: a dolly shot here, a change of camera angle there, or how to cut the scene.[22]

Rather than seeing Renoir as the single point of origin of his style, it is thus better to see it as the product of a meeting between actors' performances, the set and the camera team, all overseen by the director, the outcome of a coming together in context.

Lourié's testimony also casts important light on Renoir's attitude to studio and location shooting. If there can be little doubt that, unlike some of his contemporaries, Renoir would always choose to shoot exteriors on location, Lourié also makes it abundantly clear that both he and the director strongly preferred shooting interiors in studio conditions.[23] When discussing the set for the Wintersborn castle prison camp, for example, he writes:

> Shooting interiors in the castle was out of the question. The configuration, the size of the rooms, everything was all wrong. Moreover, Renoir preferred shooting under the controlled conditions of a stage. He was convinced, as was I, that studio sets could be more dramatically expressive and fit the story better than some actual locations. The technical ease of shooting on stage was also an irresistible advantage.[24]

This commitment to studio interiors and location-shot exteriors clearly creates a challenge when interior and exterior had to meet, as they often did in the case of a director like Renoir who so favoured composition in depth, the contextualisation of characters and the connection of spaces, often through the productive use of windows and doors. Back projection, which might have seemed the obvious solution, was ruled out because it gave a blinking and unsteady image, acceptable for shots from a moving vehicle, but not for those from within a building.[25] Lourié's ingenious solutions to the challenge are worth exploring for the light they cast on Renoir's style and for the way they problematise any over-simple understanding of his realism.

One simple solution was the use of a photograph to create the illusion of an exterior, a technique used in Renoir's *Madame Bovary* (1933) by another Russian émigré set designer Georges Wakhevitch and reused in *La Grande Illusion* for the famous dialogue between de Boeldieu and von Rauffenstein in the latter's studio-created castle room.[26] Lourié backed the room's window with a blow-up of a photograph of the real castle walls from Haut-Koenigsbourg. He reports that Renoir was impressed by how real the walls looked but remarked that if a sentry could be made to appear on the wall, the illusion would be complete. He responded by cutting out a scale, cardboard silhouette of a German soldier and moving it across the backing by hand. To the social realism of the foreground – the contextualised interaction of two aristocrats – was added the illusion of visual realism of the background. Lourié's more frequently used solution was to build an exact replica of part of the set, typically the window area, within the location or, reversing the illusion, to reconstruct part of the exterior within the studio. Both methods were used for the prisoners' room at the Hallbach camp. Because many scenes involved action happening outside the window, Lourié rebuilt part of the yard next to the room and corridor on stage (Figure 1). The floor of the room was raised to create the correct height difference between the two spaces and to allow space for the scenes where the men climb down into their tunnel.[27] One sequence of the film shows the French prisoners looking down from their room onto German recruits marching in the camp yard as they prepare their own theatrical spectacle. Here the exterior space was obviously too large to incorporate within the set and so Lourié instead built a double of the window wall on a platform at the Colmar barracks location. This allowed for the point-of-view shot through the window to be taken on location while the rest of the scene was done in the studio.[28] A similar solution was used for shots through the window at Elsa's farm. The scene where Dalio, on the inside, talks to Gabin, on the outside, was shot by bringing the window wall of the farmhouse set to the location (Figure 2).[29] Here again, the issue of realism is a complex one. If, on the one hand, Renoir's ability to film on location and to maintain spatial connections might seem a testimony to his realism, we should remember that this realism is only achieved through the very skilful sleight of hand of Lourié.

Lourié also provides precious testimony about the design and furnishing of the different sets and the mood or impression that was sought with each. For example, Elsa's farmhouse was designed, in Lourié's words, '(to) reflect a certain way of life, a simple nobility of character'.[30] The castle interiors, in contrast, are designed to express harshness. Lourié writes, 'In designing the castle sets, I tried to visually express the severity and grimness of the inaccessible stone fortress ... My dominant impression of this place was stone – stone wall and stone floors built on top of granite rock'.[31] Within the castle, von Rauffenstein's room has a special place. Lourié felt that the character would choose to live in the least confining room and so located him in the chapel, placing his bed under the large crucifix that, in Lourié's words, 'would dominate the Gothic emptiness of the chapel'.[32] The carved wood partition that Lourié added to the chapel was a real one, found after visits to a series of antique dealers.[33] If the crucifix suggested that the room was a place of suffering and sacrifice, its religious furnishings

Figure 1: The exterior brought to the interior.

Figure 2: The interior brought to the exterior.

marked it out as different from the rest of the castle, thus emphasising von Rauffenstein's isolation, an isolation further emphasised by the size of the space. Von Stroheim was apparently enchanted with the chapel set. Lourié asked him what props should be placed in it to show the imprint of his character. Stroheim gave him a three page long list of objects, including 'six pairs of white gloves, five photographs in silver frames of heavy-set blonde Wagnerian singers, the book *Casanova's Memoirs*, and more'.[34] While Renoir had to rein in Stroheim's excesses – the Wagnerian singers are not obviously apparent – Lourié's account underlines how the film's visual style resulted from a range of creative inputs. It also serves to remind us just how much characterisation in the film emerges from the props, with the austerity of the sets making the objects that express personality stand out. The mute struggle between impersonal sets and personal props can be seen as one way that the film signifies the oppressive nature of the wartime context. But of course, and as will be discussed later, the personal in 1930s Renoir is never purely individual but connects to the group and to social class.

The struggle expressed through set and props is not only over personality. It is also one between moods, between oppressive austerity and different human aspirations. It is pushed to its perhaps excessive limit when our attention is drawn to the geranium that adorns Rauffenstein's window-ledge (the only flower that grows in the castle), a symbol of beauty and perhaps love in the grim surroundings. It is present in more muted form in Lourié's design for the stables, the place where the prisoners first rehearse and then perform the theatrical show with which they express their uneasy blend of escapism and defiance. Lourié notes how 'the gloomy emptiness of the stables looked appropriate for the tense sequence of the prisoners' musical extravaganza ... the saddle holders were empty and there were no horses because they were all at the front'. He adds, however, '(t)o contrast with this gloomy emptiness, gaudy paper decorations were hung everywhere and a naively painted Eiffel Tower was used to decorate the proscenium arch.'[35] Through this conflicted appearance the set provides a suitable setting for the sharp changes of mood that occur in the entertainment sequence as well as helping sustain the contrasts that run through the visual texture of the film. In some ways the least austere sets are the ones that we find in the opening sequences of the film when first French and then German airmen are seen relaxing or celebrating in their messes. When the original idea of housing the Germans in the occupied château was abandoned, Lourié suggested that the German mess should be similar to the French one before coming to the simple but brilliant idea that they should be shot in the *same* hut.[36] The identical nature of the two spaces allowed for the development of similarities and contrasts between the two messes through the differential deployment of actors, props and decoration.

Objects, images and decors also serve to open out the time and space coordinates of the story because of their capacity to connect to a before or an elsewhere. Personal objects evoke the off-screen world of home and peace-time. Thus, for example, the pictures of horses that de Boeldieu has on the wall by his bed and the saddles and riding equipment that decorate Rauffenstein's austere chamber connect to the pre-war leisure pursuits of the aristocracy. Pictures of the Folies Bergères or the Moulin Rouge on mess walls summon up a lost Paris, a space that haunts the French cinema of the 1930s.[37]

On a larger scale, the castle itself has strong historical reverberations that will need to be explored. On a smaller scale, the pictures of brothers and a husband killed in war bring historical events into the otherwise peaceful space of Elsa's farmhouse. Historical and spatial coordinates lain down by décor and props remind us that we cannot reduce a film's spatio-temporality to the immediate space-time of the plot's unfolding.

Notes

1 Bergan, *Jean Renoir*, pp. 170–171.
2 The version of the outline I have found is type-written on Jean Renoir's own headed paper. It is held amongst his brother's papers at the Lilly Library of the University of Indiana. Although there is no way of being certain that this was the exact text passed on to Spaak for reworking, it does seem very likely.
3 Viry-Babel, 'La Grande Illusion de Jean Renoir', p. 40.
4 Choukroun, Jacques, 'A propos du premier projet de production de la Grande Illusion', *Archives* 70 (February 1997), pp. 24–26.
5 Curchod, *La Grande Illusion*, pp. 36–37.
6 The second and third drafts are held at the BIFI in Paris.
7 See http://www.haut-koenigsbourg.fr/fr (consulted 1/4/2008).
8 Lourié, Eugène, *My Work in Films* (San Diego, 1985), p. 18.
9 Curchod, Olivier, *La Grande Illusion* (Paris, 2005), pp. 14–15.
10 Lourié, *My Work in Films*, p. 19.
11 Curchod, *Jean Renoir*, p. 15.
12 Ibid., pp. 15-16.
13 Mortane, Jacques, *Evasions d'aviateurs (1914-1918)* (Paris, 1928), pp. 13-66.
14 Bazin, *Jean Renoir*, p. 59.
15 The Parisian is perhaps the most durable role, emerging in the Pinsard outline, traversing the different drafts and flowering as the actor Cartier in the film itself. The character starts life in the second, austere prison camp. By the later drafts and in the film itself, he has moved to the first camp, allowing the role to be developed in a more light-hearted context, permitting Carette to deploy his performance skills during the theatre show and sharpening the contrast between the moods of the two camps.
16 Curchod, *La Grande Illusion*, p. 40.

17 Lourié, *My Work in Films,* p. 21.

18 Curchod, *La Grande Illusion,* 2005, pp. 31–33.

19 LoBianco, Lorraine and Thompson, David (eds). *Jean Renoir, Letters* (London, 1994), pp. 31–38 (translations by C. Carlson, N. Arnoldi and M. Wells).

20 Ibid., p. 39.

21 For an account of how Lourié's set encouraged and facilitated the extreme camera mobility, connection of spaces and composition in depth of *La Règle du jeu,* see Faulkner, Christopher and Curchod, Olivier, *La Règle du jeu: scénario original de Jean Renoir* (Paris, 1999), pp. 40–43.

22 Lourié, *My Work in Films,* pp. 23–25.

23 Some of the legendary French films of the 1930s have studio-shot exteriors. René Clair's early sound, Paris trilogy of *Sous les toits de Paris* (1930), *Le Million* (1931) and *Le Quatorze juillet* (1933) is a classic example of this. Its Paris was famously built by legendary designer Lazare Meerson at the Tobis studios in Paris. Another great designer, Alexander Trauner, famously used studio space to construct the Parisian streets for Marcel Carné's late 1930s poetic realist masterpieces *Hôtel du Nord* (1938) and *Le Jour se lève* (1939). See Bergfelder, Tim, Harris, Sue and Street, Sarah, *Film Architecture and the Transnational Imagination: Set Design in 1930s European Cinema* (Amsterdam, 2007), pp. 173–183.

24 Lourié, *My Work in Films,* p. 12.

25 Ibid., p. 22.

26 Bergfelder, Harris, and Street, *Film Architecture and the Transnational Imagination,* pp. 77–78.

27 Lourié, *My Work in Films,* p. 19.

28 Ibid., p. 22.

29 Ibid., p. 29.

30 Ibid., p. 18.

31 Ibid., p. 21.

32 Ibid., p. 13.

33 Ibid., p. 26.

34 Ibid., p. 13.

35 Ibid., p. 25.

36 Ibid., p. 21.

37 Paris is the leading location of the French cinema of the 1930s and other periods. The theme of exile from it and its places of leisure and popular sociability is one that recurs in classic French films from the period like Duvivier's *Pépé le Moko* (1936) or Feyder's *Le Grand Jeu* (1933).

3 Analysis

Where should one begin an analysis of a film as rich and complex as *La Grande Illusion*. Should one start with its themes, its structure or its style? Or, recognising the limitation of looking at these elements separately, should one study their complex interplay in concrete scenes and sequences at the risk of losing sight of broader patterns? Because there is no easy answer, it is perhaps best to begin by stating briefly what the film is about before plunging into the detail. Although far from a conventional war film, it is clearly about war and ways to move beyond it. Nations and internationalism thus lie at its core. But it is also about class and how it traverses national borders while dividing nations internally. Finally, it is about history, a product of and response to a world of competing historical possibilities. History, class and nation are clearly not analytically independent themes. While class and nation cut across each other, history intervenes to remind us that their interaction is not a static one, that existing national and class boundaries can be redrawn. Without such a potential for renewal, there would be no space for a progressive political project. Renoir's Popular Front cinema is important not simply because it seeks to register the world as it is but also because it has a sense of how the world might be, no matter how narrow or difficult the path forward. But approaching the film on such an abstract level does scant justice to the stylistically rich and thematically complex ways in which it works through the issues that it addresses. A more concrete approach is now required, looking at the film's structure, its recurrent motifs, its style and its mise-en-scène of history before considering certain key scenes in detail.

Structure

The film's structure is a sensible starting point, not least because attention to its sophistication points immediately to the sharp intelligence of a work that is sometimes rather glibly seen as generous but naïve. Although the film can be divided up in a range of ways, my own preference here is to analyse its structure in terms of four acts. The first is composed of the scene in the French airmen's mess and the parallel scene in the German mess that follows the shooting down of Maréchal and de Boeldieu. The second act consists of the time spent in Hallbach, the first prison camp, where time is divided between digging an escape tunnel and the preparation and performance of a concert party. The third picks up the heroes at another camp, Wintersborn, a more sombre and austere location and ends with the escape of Maréchal and Rosenthal and the death of de Boeldieu. The final act shows the escapees' journey to the Swiss border but is dominated by the idyllic stay in Elsa's farmhouse and the burgeoning love between the German woman and Maréchal. However, any purely linear understanding of the film's structure runs the immediate risk of underestimating how its different sections combine to produce a developing commentary on war and social interaction and how it is marked by intricate patterns of repetition and contrast at the level of character, action, visual economy and sound.[1]

Because *La Grande Illusion* is a work of narrative fiction and not a cinematic essay, it is of course problematic to suggest that its structure has the shape of an argument with an introduction, a development and a conclusion. Nonetheless, something akin to an argument is implicitly developed as the film unfolds. Its first act seems to pose a set of questions while opening up possibilities for the film to explore. By inviting comparison of the French and German flyers' messes, it brings out similarities between the two groups while also showing how bonds of social class transcend national boundaries. It thus asks why war is necessary at all while inviting us to weigh the competing claims of country and class. If the opening might seem to invite us to jump to rather easy conclusions about how we might move beyond war, the second act in the Hallbach camp would seem designed to remind us of the complexity of the issues at stake and the lack of clear-sightedness of the protagonists. The French prisoners in Hallbach are in a position of enforced subordination that effectively blocks the possibilities of transnational fraternity that the opening sequences had raised. They function primarily as a national group, albeit one internally fractured by class differences. Their time is divided between preparation for escape and rehearsal for a theatrical show, two activities related to each other in complex ways. Escape would secure their liberty and rescue them from domination but would plunge them back into the war and international struggle. Theatre would seem, on the other hand, to offer a way to move away from war through playful co-operation. However, because it would neither free the men nor rescue them from domination, the escape it offered would be mere escapism. In any case, lacking clarity of vision or purpose, the Frenchmen seem unable to separate escape and escapism and treat their tunnelling as a theatrical game in a way clearly signalled when they pose and posture in front of a curtain when the tunnel is first introduced.

The interplay of escape and escapism is further complicated when news comes into the camp of the fall of Douaumont, one of the key forts protecting the historic French town of Verdun, to the Germans. Faced with the guards' vicarious celebration of triumph, the French and their English allies turn the theatrical evening into an act of implicit defiance, an attitude that becomes explicit when news of the French recapture of Verdun leads to the triumphalist singing of the 'Marseillaise'. But the allies' celebration of a gruesome massacre is no less vicarious than that of the Germans. It is quickly punctured when Maréchal, the hero, is thrown into solitary confinement and when news comes through that the Germans have again captured Douaumont, a piece of information greeted impassively by both sides, given how little must now remain of the contested fort. This part of the film underscores the grandiose hollowness of competing nationalisms while also underlining the powerful hold they have on French and German alike. While Maréchal's derisory attempt to dig his way out of solitary confinement with a spoon might seem a simple ruse to distract the guard's attention, it perhaps points at a deeper level to the sterility and inevitable frustration of any attempt to move beyond war if nationalism remains to the fore.

After the overlapping confusions of Hallbach, the third act of the film in the Wintersborn camp would seem to offer a return of clarity, not least because class tends to displace nation as the central issue, allowing a progressive politics to reassert itself, implicitly at least. Relationships are simplified as the main focus of the action shifts from the larger groups of the first camp to two couples, the aristocratic von Rauffenstein and de Boeldieu duo and the cross-class Rosenthal-Maréchal pairing. Whereas events in the first camp had culminated in sterile nationalist posturing and failed escape, the Wintersborn section climaxes with the death of de Boeldieu and, by implication, of the old social order, and the successful break-out of Maréchal and Rosenthal who together point the way towards a more democratic and egalitarian social organisation. Theatricality is still present, as an improvised concert and de Boeldieu's solo flute playing are used to provide a cover for the break-out, but it is no longer escapist in its thrust. Now put firmly in the service of liberation, it suggests a regained seriousness of intent. This change of mood is sustained by the stark austerity of the Wintersborn camp, the wintry setting and, of course, the sad death of de Boeldieu. The successful escape of Maréchal and Rosenthal invites figurative as well as literal reading. If it is clearly a physical break-out, it is perhaps also implicitly indicative of a mental breaking free as, released from the fetters of regressive nationalism, the lead characters are ready to seek some better future based on democratic and egalitarian politics.

The forth act suggests that this readiness is not complete. Faced with tiredness, cold and hunger, Maréchal lapses into a racist outburst against his Jewish escape companion. However, he quickly puts this behind him, opening the way towards the internationalist idyll at Elsa's farm. The possibility of transnational fraternity from below had been raised, of course, in the first section of the film, when Maréchal found a French-speaking German who was a mechanic like himself. But, at that stage, obstacles to that fraternity had not been explored. When the romance between the French worker and the German peasant woman again raises its possibility, the film has worked through the obstacles. It closes by sending Maréchal and Rosenthal over the border into Switzerland and, by implication, back towards the war, thus reminding us of the persisting reality of nations and bellicose nationalism. While the film is an exploration of the possible, it is also a mapping of the real. This, in part, is what makes it a model of political cinema.

Motifs

Because *La Grande Illusion* is such a rigorous working through of possibilities and obstacles to their realisation, it has of necessity a tight, organic unity with each part in some way responding to another. At the structural level, this unity expresses itself in the complex mirrorings and contrasts between the two airmen's messes of the first act and between the two prison camps of the third and forth sections. It is sustained by the longitudinal motifs that run through the film, putting flesh on the thematic bones while throwing up the multiple echoes and contrasts that make the film a complex, evolving whole. Some key motifs are worth drawing particular attention to here. These are, in the order in which they will be examined, couples and families, Christianity, food and drink, theatre and culture, language and translation.

Although, like Renoir's other Frontist films, *La Grande Illusion* is consistently concerned with groups, it also repeatedly revolves around couples that paradoxically represent both separation from the collective and an intensification of its dynamics, couples always pointing to something beyond themselves. Firstly, there is the Maréchal-Joséphine couple of the start, one which suggests a peaceful and non-possessive coming together, but one condemned not to occur by the war. Then, there are the couples that war throws up, the tragic, aristocratic de Boeldieu-von Rauffenstein duo, which encapsulates the position of their broader class, and the Maréchal-Rosenthal pairing, embodying egalitarian cross-class alliance. Finally, there is the Maréchal-Elsa couple of the final act which, echoing but replacing the abortive Maréchal-Joséphine couple suggests a peaceful overcoming of national borders. Always raising broad questions of human interconnectedness, couples thus play a considerable role in developing the film's key themes of class and nation. Within the series of couples, it is no doubt significant that only the final one opens out onto a temporary (non-biological) family as constituted by Maréchal, Elsa, Rosenthal and the child Lotte. This unconventional unit arises in the place where Elsa's original and more conventional family had lived before war killed the men whose portraits, so many markers of absence, hang on the wall. Elsa's lost family was German and Christian. Her new, temporary family is international and cross-faith. If the ethnically homogenous family serves to tie human belonging to the nation, and to justify sometimes murderous exclusions, the closing group opens the family onto less bounded and destructive possibilities.

Couples in the film are not only used to explore issues of nation and class. They also invite us to engage with gendered relations and identities while reminding us that a film which seems to accord little space to women is also haunted by them – note the many photographs of women on the walls – and not a little anxious about them. The Joséphine evoked in the opening scene would seem to be the model of the woman whom men are happy to share and thus serves to sustain male-bonding while guaranteeing male heterosexuality. She finds her echo in Fifi, the woman that both the aristocrats remember 'knowing' in pre-war Paris. Had earlier versions of the script remained unchanged, she would also have been echoed by the German peasant woman whom Maréchal and Rosenthal's precursor, Dolette, were to have shared in another 'safe' expression of tight male bonding. However, Joséphine has a disturbing counterpart, another absent female, the woman left behind who betrays her husband.[2] The schoolteacher of the first camp shows repeated concern over his wife's infidelity, a behaviour that seems to condense a broader sense that women have escaped male control and, not least because of their very changed appearances, are no longer what they were. Tellingly, discussion at Wintersborn associates female sexual activity with the spread of venereal diseases, in a way that seems light-hearted on the surface but which again suggests a lurking anxiety. While the shared woman serves above all as a reassuring 'marker' for the men, the sexually active one who escapes their control is far more worrying. Reviewed in this light, the closing heterosexual romance might seem a retreat to the safely familiar, locking the woman back into her domestic role as mother and partner. However, it could also be seen in more optimistic terms as a reconciliation of male and female agencies and desires. Elsa is clearly a desiring subject. Echoing the film's many images of absent women, the photographs on her wall point to the gap left in her life by the loss of husband and brothers, something underscored when she points out the unoccupied chairs around the dining table and when she later remarks how much pleasure it has given her to hear Maréchal's manly footsteps in her house. Seen in this way, the Maréchal-Elsa couple might be seen not only as a Franco-German reconciliation but also as progressive vision of the couple that gave full recognition to female desire. Elsa might then take her place alongside the Valentine of *Le Crime de Monsieur Lange* as one of Renoir's admirable, desiring female subjects.[3] But one should not of course forget how, as we noted in our study of the film's genesis, the building of a meaningful part for her was contingent on the casting of Parlo and did not flow automatically from some pre-existing design. Nor can we be sure of the reasons behind the non-appearance in the film of the sadistic temptress who had played a prominent role in successive drafts of the script.

Alongside gender, religion is clearly another important longitudinal thread. If Christianity seems largely absent from the first prison camp, reference to it would seem to be implicitly made when the cadastrial engineer played by Gaston Modot washes Maréchal's feet, a gesture with clear biblical resonance suggestive of a Christian ethic of care. It becomes more prominent at Wintersborn in the shape of the massive crucifix that dominates von Rauffenstein's room, the old castle chapel, and in the form of the priest who brings the last rights to the dying de Boeldieu. The crib of the final act, a symbol of rebirth, is clearly a form of answer to the Crucifix with its associations of death, suffering and sacrifice.[4] The earlier footwashing is also echoed in the final act when Elsa prepares to bathe Rosenthal's injured foot. Christianity amplifies the resonance of some of the film's chief events (such as the sacrifice of de Boeldieu) and supports its thematic texture by providing a ready-made pan-European internationalism. But it would nevertheless be a mistake to see it as a Christian film. De Boeldieu may indeed die for others in a Christ-like way, but the film invites us to see his act in more all-embracing, mythical terms. His name is a condensation of '*de bois-le-dieu*,' the 'God of the woods'. It is no accident that he wears a goat-skin flying coat and later uses a flute to distract the Germans while his comrades escape. He is as reminiscent of the pagan god Pan as of Christ. The use of Christianity is strategic as is underscored by the crib scene near the end when the Jewish Rosenthal reminds us that Jesus is his 'racial' brother. In the same way as the film opens the family onto international diversity, the linking of Rosenthal with Jesus opens Christianity onto a plurality of beliefs. Even as the film taps into core elements of the contemporary world (family, religion) it reworks their significance to suit its progressive purpose and to embed its opposition to fascism.

While the Christianity embedded in the film's action and visual fabric endows it with a certain symbolic weightiness, it is leavened by the presence of two more 'frivolous' longitudinal threads, food and theatre. The sharing of food and drink runs through a film that has many more scenes of eating than of fighting. Food has many associations. Although the group meal is the film's preferred way to show its attachment to warm, fraternal community and egalitarian sharing, food also serves to put flesh on the bones of the potentially abstract concepts of class and nation. The two aristocrats and the rich French Jew have frequented Maxim's and Le Fouquet's, luxurious Parisian haunts. In contrast, the proletarian Maréchal prefers a simple bistro and an ordinary table wine while the humble school teacher can only afford to eat at his brother-in-law's when in Paris. If eating thus divides the French along class lines, it also pulls them together in the shared love of food and drink, a stereotypical national trait demonstrated in the 'banquet' scene in the first camp. The guards, in contrast, are seen consuming cabbage, a stereotypically German dish that serves both to underscore national differences and to point to the difficulties a blockaded Germany faced feeding its population during the war. Food serves more broadly to ground characters' lives in the material world. Thus, the failure of the French to address the harsh realities of war in the first camp is underscored by the sumptuous fare that they consume. Bringing him down to earth, Maréchal's solitary confinement confronts him with hunger, a sensation he will again have to face during his trek towards the Swiss border with Rosenthal, making a real sacrifice in pursuit of freedom. The hospitality shown by Elsa is similarly marked at the material level when she feeds the hungry Maréchal when he first arrives at her house. Her simple generosity contrasts with the Russian Czarina's failure to address the material needs of the Russian prisoners in Wintersborn when she sends them books instead of the food and drink that they expect. Shared food and drink and celebratory meals are favoured Renoir motifs and remind us that Renoir is a film-maker of the concrete and the physical. The film's core themes of nation, class, war and history could potentially lend themselves to a dry, purely intellectual treatment. But food helps ensure that they are grounded in the material and in the everyday so that fraternity is no mere idea but a warm, embodied sharing.

Theatricality is another favourite Renoir motif in both its specific dimension as stage performance and its more diffuse mode as enactment of social role. If, like food, it might seem to have a purely ludic dimension, the way it is used also reminds us of the film's rigour. In its narrower form as stage performance, it gives the film a strong element of reflexivity, inviting us to ponder the relationship between spectacle and nationalism. This happens most clearly during the concert sequence in the first camp. Before the concert, the frivolous and disrespectful performances of Cartier, the actor, or the dancing of the English soldiers in drag apparently represent a polar opposite and challenge to the hierarchy, discipline and restraint of the German guards. The concert complicates this sense of opposition by showing how even apparently frivolous performance can be sucked into the conflict. It also invites us to ponder our own role as spectators of popular entertainment. This is something to which we will return. The more diffuse theatricality of social roles is something here associated with the upper classes, as in other Renoir films like *La Marseillaise*, *Les Bas-fonds* or *La Règle du jeu*.[5] Both de Boeldieu and von Rauffenstein are dandies whose performances of nobility suggest the decadence and narcissism of a condemned caste. Their stiffness and mannerisms and monocles and white gloves all separate them out from the other characters, making them the embodiment of social distinction in a way that helps downplay differences between the others.

If, when tied to bodily posture, to clothes, to manners, identity is rooted in the concrete and the everyday and made more solid, it is simultaneously and paradoxically made less permanent. Because it exists partly at the level of performance, it is open to reworking and to re-enactment in the same way that actors can change role, costume or gesture. The potential for change is thus also written into the material fabric of the film. This is perhaps most obvious in the theatrical rehearsal and show when the men cross-dress, something apparently frivolous on the surface but that points, at a deeper level, to the destabilisation of gender relations brought about by the war, a change underscored when the prisoners discuss the shifting boundaries between male and female appearances. Later, we learn that Maréchal has sought to escape dressed as a woman, thereby attracting the unwanted sexual interest of a German soldier. Thus unsettled at the level of appearance, the established script of masculinity is also reworked at a more general level by the behaviour of the prisoners within the camp. While the war drives them to fight, the camp sees them cook, iron and care for each other to the point that Rosenthal cries when Maréchal is released from solitary confinement. Taking things a stage further, the platonic relationship between von Rauffenstein and de Boeldieu is part seduction, part tragic romance. Overall, the questioning of male and female roles is clearly double edged. If it suggests a clear sense of anxiety, it also opens up the possibility of new forms of masculinity less tied to struggle and more open to nurture and care.

Exploration of theatricality can usefully be broadened to embrace the cultural more generally. Unsurprisingly, in what is one of the key films of the Popular Front period, it is popular culture that shows the capacity to pull people together. This is in evidence from the very first scene where Maréchal sings along to a popular song, 'Frou frou', while around him other French airmen share food and drink. The same song builds a fragile transnational bridge when Maréchal plays it on the mouth organ while in solitary confinement and the old German guard sings along. Popular songs like 'Marguerite' and 'It's a long way to Tipperary' show a similarly utopian capacity to join classes and nations together during the concert party before chauvinism intervenes. Later, another song, 'Il était un petit navire' will draw the French and Russians together in a performance that will prepare for the escape of Maréchal and Rosenthal. Performed again by de Boeldieu as he distracts the guards' attention, it will also serve to allow the escapees to work through their mutual frustration at the low point of their trek towards the border. Not always festive or immune from nationalist co-optation, the popular always has a collective dimension that allows it to transcend boundaries and create communities, however short-lived. To the degree that it is in evidence, high art is more associated with private individuals. Thus, for example, Rosenthal has a Botticelli print, a culturally validated object that marks him out from other characters, by his bed in both camps, while von Rauffenstein has a volume of Heine, the German poet, among the eclectic display of possessions in his chapel room, an object that again signals his difference to others. More noticeably, the teacher at Wintersborn is engaged in a translation of the ancient Greek poet, Pindar. His declaration that Pindar is more important than the war, than them, than everything, seems fatuous in the light of the context. While the popular opens characters out onto the collective, high culture seems to lock them into the self.

As the son of a great Impressionist painter and someone who had grown up in a house visited by great cultural figures such as the writer Zola, Renoir was far from a stranger to the world of high culture. However, *La Grande Illusion* shows a commitment to the popular that can be connected both to the Popular Front context and to the director's dedication to the twentieth century's most important popular art form. But just as his repeated depiction of eating should not be too reductively connected to an epicurean love of life, his commitment to the popular should not be seen as facile populism. In his hands and those of his collaborators, far from giving people the already known, the cliché, the prejudice or the comfort of the familiar, the popular is inhabited and transformed by the political. In return it serves as a vehicle to take the political to a larger audience. For politics to inhabit the popular, translations of course have to occur. This is in part the role played by some of the longitudinal motifs that we have looked at which serve to take the political into the everyday and the concrete thus enabling it to speak to embodied experience.

Translation is itself a recurrent motif in a film famed for its realistic interplay of a range of languages. Like food or culture, language both brings people together and keeps them apart. Linguistic diversity is one of the main ways in which national difference manifests itself in the film, corralling people into apparently natural groups, impeding communication between them. But translation and multilingualism build bridges and denaturalise divisions. The most famous case is the ability of the two aristocrats to converse in both French and English, bringing their shared class identity to the fore. A foreign tongue for both men, the latter language provides, as Michel Chion notes, a neutral terrain upon which they can meet while underlining the cosmopolitanism of the social elite.[6] But linguistic mobility is far from limited to the aristocracy. Rosenthal, the Jew born in Vienna, speaks French and German. A Russian is seen giving a lesson in his native tongue to a Frenchman at the start of the Hallbach section. The German flyer who has worked in the Gnome factory in France speaks French as do some of the guards. All these show that commoners can also break down the barriers of language. But such a phenomenon is not necessarily progressive. As the example of the guards shows, translation can simply be a tool through which one group exercises control over another. For the utopian potential of language learning and translation to be realised, domination has to be removed. This is what happens at Elsa's farm when Maréchal, who had seemed trapped in a monolingual prison, finally makes progress in German. He comments that while the guards' German defeated him, Elsa's makes sense. 'Verboten' ('forbidden'), a word repeatedly heard in the camps, and mocked subversively by Maréchal, can now be spoken in simple good humour when Maréchal tells Elsa's daughter Lotte that she is not allowed to eat the baby Jesus.

If translation and multilingualism can break down the frontiers between languages, different class codes and accents fragment them internally. De Boeldieu's use of language is as mannered as the rest of his behaviour. When he volunteers to do his share of the tunnelling, he ironically but pompously comments, 'I've heard it said that crawling is a most salutary exercise', thus underlining his linguistic distance from the other characters even as he offers to help them. At other times, his use of the formal 'vous' indicates the barrier he wishes to maintain between himself and others, something that the informal 'tu' would have diminished. His English conversation with von Rauffenstein before the latter is obliged to shoot him is an incongruous model of controlled politeness. Maréchal, in contrast, speaks the familiar Parisian French of the working classes, a code that seems instinctively egalitarian in its lack of pretension. Language thus follows similar patterns to other motifs. Criss-crossed by differences of class and nationality, it can also traverse barriers to pull people together, thus bringing progressive possibilities to the fore while reminding us of barriers to their realisation.

Film style and group dynamics

There is a temptation to stop at the surface of La Grande Illusion and to simply admire its stylistic mastery. But we need to go further and to explore the relationship between style and meaning, form and content if we are to do justice to the greatness of the film. As noted earlier, Renoir's mature style of the later 1930s is characterised by a refusal to separate behaviours from their social and physical contexts that manifests itself in long takes, a mobile camera, composition in depth and a preference for shots of groups. This style reaches a high-point of perfection with *La Grande Illusion* and serves as an ideal vehicle for the film's exploration of the interaction of class and national belongings.

By my reckoning, there are just over 350 shots in a film that lasts 107 minutes, which means that the average shot length is just over eighteen seconds, significantly longer than the 12.5 seconds that Colin Crisp gives as the norm for the period and much longer than the typical 7–10 second average shot length of contemporaneous Hollywood films.[7] The film has relatively few very short takes. Only about 17 per cent of the shots are three seconds or less and just over 50 per cent ten seconds or less, meaning that very nearly 50 per cent are more than ten seconds, with about 30 per cent more than twenty seconds and about 20 per cent half a minute or more. There are ten shots of more than a minute. These figures only suggest a balance between longer and shorter takes if we forget that the about 50 per cent of shots of more than ten seconds represent very considerably more than 50 per cent of screen time. The film is predominantly made up of quite long and very long takes. One might in fact say that the latter is dominant, with shots of over half a minute taking up nearly an hour. Furthermore, strengthening this dominance, extreme long takes tend to occupy strategic points in the film, often serving to establish locations and the social and spatial relations within them.[8] This begins from the very first shot of the film when a take of nearly a minute is used to introduce the French airmen's mess and the relationships and activities within it. Following the same pattern, we are introduced to the German flyer's mess with two takes of about a minute each. When actions shift to Hallbach, the shot of the post-room that introduces a new group of characters is more than a minute, while the first shot of the interior of the prisoners' room is little short of a minute and the shot that introduces the tunnelling and people's role within it is an astonishing bravura long take of nearly two minutes. When we move to the Wintersborn camp, a shot of nearly seventy seconds explores von Rauffenstein's room and the objects within it. Modifying but not breaking the pattern, shots that introduce spaces and actions at Elsa's farms are still extended if less long. The first interior shot of the farmhouse is a little over half a minute. The brief scene that shows Maréchal feeding the cow in the byre is shown in a single take of over forty seconds, while the Christmas crib sequence is introduced with another shot of similar length.

Calling the very extended takes that tend to introduce spaces and actions 'establishing' shots is both deceptive and illuminating. It is deceptive in that, unlike conventional establishing shots which place us at a significant distance from the action or the characters and are often static, these shots put us into the space of the action and are usually highly mobile. It is illuminating in that it points to how these shots are used to establish spaces, objects and characters and the relationships between them. They are, one might say, an affirmation of connectivity and of the way in which social contexts are always already present in actions. The shots may begin with a close-up or medium shot of an object or a person, but tracking backwards or sideways, panning left or right, tilting up or down, exploiting the characteristic depth of field, they refuse the isolation or, equally as important, the prioritisation of a person or thing as they explore a space from within.[9] A good example is the first shot of the film (Figure 3). It begins with a close-up of a gramophone as the song 'Frou frou' is heard. It tilts upwards to show us Maréchal's face in close-up as, behind him, out of focus, other aviators take their seats around a table. The camera pans right and brings tables and the bar into focus, following Maréchal as he moves across the room to ask a comrade for a lift. When he moves left again, the camera remains still, picks up the squadron leader as he enters the room and follows him back to join Maréchal at the gramophone. The two are held in medium shot as Maréchal receives his orders and the camera again tracks right as they move back across the room towards the door behind a group of aviators eating at one of the tables. While Maréchal, the hero, and his senior officer are the two principal characters here, both are presented as part of the broader context of the French mess and the way people interact within it. Were the same people, objects and actions to have been presented through conventional analytical editing in a series of separate shots or without the composition in depth, they would have tended to become detached from the whole. Or, rather, the relationship between the whole and the parts would have been altered. Whereas the long, mobile take subordinates the part to the whole, analytical editing reverses the relationship. The kind of Bazinian understanding of such a shot that we discussed earlier would emphasize how it respects the ontological unity of the world. A more political understanding would note how the shot prioritised social relations and contexts over individuals and isolated actions.

Figure 3: The connectivity and shifting centres of interest of the opening long take.

The way the opening shot treats the gramophone is repeated with variations at different stages of the film where a recurrent procedure is to begin with a close-up of an object before moving backward to widen the framing and to take in people, spaces and things. Tying the object into its context, such staging also allows the object to flavour all that is embraced by the same shot, thus creating a unity of mood. An example is the long, sinuous panning and tracking shot that explores von Rauffenstein's castle room. The shot begins with the crucifix (Figure 4) before setting off on an exploration of a disparate series of possessions that will eventually lead to their owner. The odd one out amongst the objects, belonging to the room rather than its occupant, the cross nonetheless colours all that we see there with a sense of suffering that will inflect not only how we see the German but also how we later perceive the death of de Boeldieu in the same space. In contrast, the long take that presents the Christmas crib at Elsa's begins with a close up of the tinsel wound round the wooden sticks that make up the simple roof of the stable (Figure 5). The combination of simplicity and festivity sets the tone for what follows.

Figure 4: Gothic gloom and suffering.

Figure 5: Festive simplicity.

If many of the shots that begin with a close-up of an object form a subset of the 'establishing' long takes that are distributed through the film, there are other very long takes that do not play the same establishing role. These often occur at particular moments of tension or crisis and work to underscore the interaction of groups. A striking example, a shot of just under a minute, is when news comes through of the capture by the Germans of the key French fort of Douaumont. Beginning with a close-up of the communiqué that announces the event, the camera pans right to show the guards celebrating through a window, tracks back, pans again to follow a guard as he exits the room, still celebrating, and follows him as he passes under another window from which the French prisoners are watching the triumphant Germans. Several separate shots could have recounted the same actions. The beauty of the way Renoir handles it in a single mobile take is to bring out the unity of the moment, underscoring how the triumph of one group is inextricably tied to the defeat of another. The shot is answered by another of similar length and mobility when news comes through of the French recapture of Douaumont during the concert party and the English officer leads the singing of the 'Marseillaise'. Beginning with a medium group view of the musicians, the shot pans right into a close-up of the Englishman, then tracks back, panning further right and tilting up to give a low angle shot of Maréchal and Rosenthal singing triumphantly on the stage. It then moves behind the German officers to pick up their reaction in close-up, pans again to pick up the front row of the audience, tracks forward to again show the smiling Englishman singing and, finally, pans left again to face the audience front row also singing. Again emphasising through its unity the inevitable link between one group's triumph and another's defeat, the shot also underscores how individuals are part of social contexts. Close-ups classically detach characters' reactions from what surrounds them. Renoir's ability to incorporate them in complex long takes that track group interaction reinserts the individual and the emotional into the collective context.

The film has many other long takes that are neither as extended nor as striking as those just discussed but which nevertheless underscore the same formal choices. Typically showing group interaction and featuring camera mobility, they often shift their centre of interest by moving from one individual or cluster of characters to another. These shifts of focus could be seen as the structural equivalent of cross-cutting except that, by avoiding editing, they underscore the simultaneity and connectivity of what is shown, always rooting individual and group actions in a broader context.

As Bazin has noted, the natural complement to the lateral mobility of Renoir's framing is the typically in-depth composition of the image. *La Grande Illusion* is no exception in this respect as its shots are often composed on two or more planes in a way that ensures the social and spatial contextualisation of foreground events while emphasising the interactions of groups. A typical type of shot in the Hallbach part of the film is one that confronts a line of prisoners with the German officers giving them orders. One such shot that shows the initial 'welcome' of the group of prisoners in which Maréchal finds himself is composed on four planes. Two guards in the foreground flank an officer in the middle ground as he tells the prisoners further into the image that they must report to his office (Figure 6). As they all leave the frame, they reveal a line of young German soldiers who are receiving their training in the background (Figure 7). The in-depth composition (and the use of the guards to frame the image) shows how one nationality confronts, contains and dominates another. At the same time, the prisoners' enforced passivity is contrasted with the active preparation for war behind them.

At other times, the depth of the frame is used to remind us of the presence of guards behind the French even as they entertain themselves or relax. The guards are typically seen through the windows or doorways that Renoir so often uses to connect one space to another. Thus, for example, during the sequence which shows the French eating sumptuously at Hallbach, we repeatedly see guards at the back of the image (Figure 8). If the group interaction in the foreground shows the enjoyment of food that unites the French and the class differences that divide them, the background presence of the guards reminds us of the broader context of domination and imprisonment which gives a sense of frivolity to what we see in the foreground. Other similar shots at Hallbach connect the prisoners' room, in the foreground, with young German soldiers training in the courtyard in the background, with the haphazard order of one group brought into contrast with the military discipline of the other. Establishing a different relation between inside and outside, some shots at Elsa's farm allow interior space to open onto the hillside and valley beyond. Contrasting with the enclosed, disciplinary spaces of the camp, these shots emphasise the freedom enjoyed at the farm. We should remember, of course, that such shots were heavily dependent on Lourié's ability to build sets within which different spaces connected. It is no accident either that the great majority of the long, mobile takes that so characterise the film are to be found in the studio built sets that the designer made for the film and owe their existence to the flexibility that such sets allowed.

Figure 6: Three planes ...

Figure 7: ... that were hiding a fourth.

The film's laterally mobile framing and in-depth composition are complemented by the ability of off-screen sound to activate unseen spaces and remind us that what we see on screen is part of something larger than itself. Even when we cannot see the German troops training at Hallbach, for example, we can sometimes hear them. Similarly, when we first see von Rauffenstein in his chamber at Wintersborn, we hear bugles in the background inviting us to connect him to the broader context of

Figure 8: Easy conviviality in the foreground, but with a guard in the background in the lower-middle pane.

the military machine. When the French are rather theatrically preparing to tunnel at Hallbach, Maréchal's attention to off-screen noises reminds us of the broader camp context and of a danger that undercuts the on-screen lightness. Along similar lines, the military song sung by the unseen group of young soldiers that passes Elsa's house serves to remind us that military preparations continue even as what we see within the house opens the possibility of something radically different. Through its ability to connect different spaces and activities, off-screen sound repeatedly helps the film root actions in contexts that explain what we see on screen or develop important contrasts with it.

We can now identify with reasonable precision the dominant stylistic pattern in *La Grande Illusion* and its relationship to the film's thematic content. Focussing on collective dynamics rather than individuals, starting from connectivity and contextualisation rather than fragmentation and isolation, it is a style that lends itself perfectly to the film's exploration of nation and class, of what divides and what unites people. The film is not of course stylistically uniform and other patterns are seen but, where they do occur, they are best seen as divergences from the more general norm. For example, if we begin by noting that, consistent with other preferences, Renoir generally handles conversation by filming characters as a group, using the mobile camera to shift the centre of interest as necessary, we can better understand those passages that resort to the shot-reverse shot approach that was the dominant norm in classical Hollywood. One such passage occurs during the short interchange when the engineer asks Maréchal whether de Boeldieu can be trusted. The film cuts between the pair, emphasising the potential difference between them, until Maréchal convinces his comrade that the aristocrat is reliable. The two are then framed together in tight close-up, the gap between them abolished, as the engineer takes Maréchal into his confidence about the escape plans. The shot reverse-shot style is used in the most developed way for the conversation between von Rauffenstein and de Boeldieu in the former's Wintersborn chamber. Rather than using an extended two-shot as one might have expected given the many things the aristocrats share, the film chooses to cut repeatedly between the two in a way that underlines politico-historical disagreement rather than social proximity. In contrast, the shot that immediately follows the scene is an extended two-shot of more than a minute showing Maréchal and Rosenthal cementing their cross-class alliance.

Other variations from the film's dominant style are more banal in origin. Thus, there is a marked acceleration in the film's cutting rate during the successful escape. Needing to follow the movements and reactions of different groups of guards, the massed prisoners, the escapees, von Rauffenstein and de Boeldieu, the film shifts to cross-cutting, which, combined with the acceleration of the action, drastically reduces the average shot length. The rapidest cutting in the film occurs here when there are three shots of about a second of different German soldiers firing rifles. Immediately de Boeldieu has been shot, the film slows dramatically with a shot of nearly a minute of von Rauffenstein and the guards giving way to the solemn succession of long takes that show de Boeldieu's death.

The mobility and shifting centre of interest of many shots militate against orderly and symmetrical compositions. Again, when such variations from the norm do occur, there is a good reason for them. Thus, for example, just before the Wintersborn prisoners stage the improvised concerto that lays the ground for the escape, there is a shot in a guardroom that is strikingly symmetrical in its composition. There is a table in the centre of the frame on which stands a wine bottle flanked by two glasses. On either edge of it sit two German officers. One talks to the other of the benefits of German order, something encapsulated by the shot itself (Figure 9). As they talk, the off-screen sounds of the impromptu concert break the calm of the room, drawing the two to the window, disrupting the original composition. Much less orderly, ensuing shots follow the chaotic movements generated by the prisoners' revolt (Figure 10).

Figure 9: Symmetrical order

Figure 10: Liberatory chaos

Much earlier in the film, back in the German flyer's mess, there is a consecutive pair of strikingly symmetrical shots. The first frames von Rauffenstein and de Boeldieu as they eat. Behind and above them, there is a portrait of the Kaiser on the wall in centre frame. The triangular

composition that results suggests the hierarchical social organisation of the
old social order, with ruler at its peak and aristocracy below (Figure 11). The
next shot begins in equally symmetrical fashion, framing Maréchal and the
German airman who has worked in France on either side of a picture of a
woman at the same height as them (Figure 12). The class equivalence of the
two men is suggested but this time without the sense of a pyramidal social
hierarchy. In both prison camps, as in the German mess and the guardroom
just discussed, images recur in which figures are seen in front of and below
portraits of the Kaiser or military commanders, repeatedly reminding us of
the presence of an unequal and authoritarian social order.

Figure 11: A pyramidal social structure

Figure 12: Informal egalitarianism

The struggle between hierarchical order and egalitarian disorder continues through the disposition of bodies within the frame. If the film prefers the group to the individual, not all groups are equivalent. The Hallbach camp repeatedly offers us images of young soldiers in orderly blocks performing military exercises under the command of officers (Figure 13). The French prisoners are typically grouped in unstructured clusters (Figure 14) that can of course become a line when nations are set against each other, either when the prisoners are lined up facing their gaolers or when the inmates' mood becomes defiant, as when they pull themselves to attention to sing the 'Marseillaise'. The same tensions of course play over individual bodies as they stand to attention, pull themselves defiantly to their feet, straggle, lounge or cross-dress. We discussed von Rauffenstein's stiff bearing earlier in relation to the Austrian or Prussian officer stereotype that was von Stroheim's stock-in-trade. But the same bearing should also be seen as part of the more general militarisation and disciplining of the male body seen throughout the film, notably but not only in the training sequences. While we might be tempted to see the cross-dressed male body as the antithesis of this virile masculinity, we should remember how quickly the Englishman in drag pulls of his wig and draws himself into a virile pose as he leads the 'Marseillaise'.

La Grande Illusion can be seen as one of the pinnacles of the work of 1930s Renoir, an exemplary illustration of how wonderfully his style enabled the exploration of group dynamics and social relations. If its deployment of interlocking motifs allows it to put flesh on its exploration of the interaction of class and nation, its style allows the same interaction and the interplay of different forms of group dynamic to take visual and audible shape. Yet, as I have underlined, the film does not simply represent a static picture of the tensions it explores. It shows a world that is subject to change and so its mise-en-scène of social relations is also the mise-en-scène of history. The film is not just shot in deep space. It is also shot in deep time.

Shooting in deep time

There are two histories present in *La Grande Illusion*, the finished and apparently unchanging history of pastness and the ongoing, mutable and

Figure 13: Disciplined bodies ...

Figure 14: ... and disorderly groups.

malleable history that is still unfolding. The former is easily found at the
surface of the film. Set in the First World War, needing to be seen to be
faithful to documented events and behaviours, the film could hardly not
be seen to respect it if it were to be taken seriously in a country where so
many had died, known combat or been indelibly marked by events. The
latter, the history still being shaped at the time of fascism and the Popular
Front, had to hide itself were the film not to be seen to have betrayed the
former, the history that had finished. It would nonetheless make itself felt
in the film's visual and auditory fabric, in its décor and mise-en-scène and,

of course, in the web of historical references embedded in its dialogue. One does not have to dig too far to find how the film reaches back before the First World War: the singing of the 'Marseillaise', the revolutionary anthem, and reference to the French Revolution in discussions between de Boeldieu and von Rauffenstein would be enough to invite us to situate events in a longer historical unfolding did not the presence of the two aristocrats as representatives of a still unfinished European 'ancien régime' already push us in that direction. The fact that the Wintersborn camp is a mediaeval castle is another invitation to take a long-term view of the past. But, one might still wonder how the action of the film could be made to look beyond itself to engage with the threat of fascism and further war while registering the potential for historical progress. The beginnings of an answer can be found in something we have already noted; that is, how the film explores, as it unfolds, the tension between the real and the possible and thus opens the space of the future. But the beginnings now need building upon.

A good place to start is the first sequence of the film, where Maréchal is singing along with the gramophone recording of 'Frou frou'. 'Frou frou' is a doubly nostalgic song. Composed before the war, it clearly connects back to a time of peace before the conflict. Yet referring to a period when women were wearing trousers to ride bicycles and expressing its own preference for 'real' women in frilly petticoats, it looks back to an even earlier time whose stability was encapsulated in clearly demarcated gender identities. When Maréchal is torn away from the song by his wartime duties as a flyer, it is as if he had fallen into history and a world of irrevocable change. As if to confirm this, discussion amongst the Hallbach prisoners of the new woman that the war brings reveals that the stability that apparently fixed gender identities seemed to offer has been lost. The world is mutable. 'Frou frou' is heard again when it is played by Maréchal in solitary confinement even as the German guard hums along with him. If in some ways it now seems even more nostalgically turned to the past, inevitably reminding us of the period before the airman's capture, it also opens timidly onto the future by showing how Frenchman and German could come together were circumstances different.

While 'Frou frou' suggests a nostalgia that is democratic and peaceful if not without its own gendered oppressions, the obsessive 'presence' of absent horses suggests something less peaceful and less inclusive. First raised in the early conversation between the two aristocrats, the horses populate the empty stables turned theatre at Hallbach and decorate the wall above de Boeldieu's bed, before haunting von Rauffenstein's Wintersborn room in the shape of saddles, stirrups and riding whips. By their absence the horses signal the end of the 'romantic' nineteenth century mode of war. They also announce the end of the caste that routinely provided the cavalry with its officers, except that this class, which Renoir knew so well due to his time as a dragoon, seems to linger despite its time being passed.

If 'Frou frou' and the horses primarily connect to history through a sense of nostalgia and loss, the 'Marseillaise' sung at Hallbach comes with much weightier baggage due to its evocation of the French revolutionary heritage. When it is heard, that heritage seems to have lost its way. Triggered by the French recapture of Douaumont and replying to the celebratory singing of 'Die Wacht am Rhein' ('Watch on the Rhine') by the guards, the song is a model of ambiguity. Sung by defiant prisoners to their guards, it retains a still live connection to the revolutionary tradition. But, to the degree that it has been sucked into a murderous, self-perpetuating and self-defeating Franco-German rivalry, it suggests that the French have lost sight of its revolutionary dimension, blinded by the nationalist baggage it also carried. Verdun was a battle that came to encapsulate the war due to the senseless slaughter associated with it. Its coupling with the 'Marseillaise' (the battle song of the French army of the Rhine) broadens its resonance still further, making it stand in for the longer term struggle between France and Germany of which the Great War was simply one round.

Confirming the sense that any meaningful sense of history is threatened with collapse, the Wintersborn prison camp seems to represent both a dystopian future and a past that refuses to die away. The camp's austere and repressive regime looks forward to twentieth century totalitarianisms and notably to what was emerging in Germany in the 1930s. But at the same time, because it is a mediaeval fortress presided over by an aristocrat, it suggests a lurch back into a pre-revolutionary past. It is in this context that de Boeldieu's death acquires its full resonance. When the French aristocrat sacrifices himself so that a proletarian and a bourgeois Jew may together break free, he is not simply making a political choice in favour of democracy and equality, he is also showing how sense and direction can only be given back to history if the war signals the final end of the European old regimes and the shift to a new egalitarian order. But of course this is only one possible historical outcome. Von Rauffenstein suggests another. A relic of the old regime, a mediaeval survivor, an erstwhile knight of the sky, he puts himself in the service of a regimented prison system, just as members of Germany's traditional elite were to become collaborators with the Nazi regime. It is perhaps no accident that the portrait of Hindenburg sits on the old chapel altar in his castle room.[10] German commander-in-chief for part of the war, he would be president when Hitler came to power, a symbol of the ungodly collaboration between the old, undemocratic elite and the new, fascist order. When Maréchal and Rosenthal break out of the castle, leaping into the night, they are literally moving from one history to another.

It is no doubt significant that the song that accompanies their escape is one without an existing politics. 'Il était un petit navire' is a traditional song with religious overtones. It recounts the story of a little boat whose starving occupants draw lots to decide who will be eaten. The youngest on board is selected. He offers up a prayer to the Virgin Mary and is saved when thousands of little fish jump into the boat. In the absence of a suitable political anthem – absorbed by bellicose nationalism, the 'Marseillaise' is clearly not available – the film has to politicise and historicise another song. Often sung by groups on outings, 'Un petit navire' is eminently suitable for the festive, disruptive prison camp performance that covers the escape. But at the same time, due to its story of threatened human sacrifice, it connects both to the war (a continent devouring its young) and to de Boeldieu's self-sacrifice for the group. In this first version it suggests a tragic view of history in which some must die so that others may go forward. It is heard again when Maréchal seems about to abandon the injured Rosenthal on the mountainside. History seems to be locked into a cycle of repetition with another sacrifice threatened. However, in a way typical of the Popular Front Renoir, the film refuses the fatalism of predestination. The memory of sacrifice helps prevent its repetition, maintaining an opening to the future. The use of 'Un petit navire' thus echoes that of 'Frou frou'. Whereas songs in some key French films of the 1930s seemed locked into the search for a lost past (an original performance, a happier time, a united group), the repeated songs of *La Grande Illusion* can serve as vectors of memory yet still open onto the future. Each enactment of them being different, they develop their own dynamic of repetition and change. Part of the film's occupation of the terrain of popular culture, they help illustrate the kind of transformation to which the popular has to be submitted to become politically useful.

Rather than a simple linear unfolding, La Grande Illusion is the mise-en-scène of competing historical possibilities as expressed through a complex choreography of groups and bodies to a rich musical score. In this context, the section of the film at Elsa's farm is best appreciated as the development of a possibility of whose fragility the film-maker is fully aware. Its bringing together of the German peasant woman, the French proletarian and the bourgeois Jew expresses a commitment to egalitarian internationalism and a refusal of the monstrous desire for ethnic purity tormenting the Europe of the 1930s. Yet, while the film suggests that this generous path forward is available at the time of the Popular Front, it also reminds us of darker possibilities, as when the German soldiers march past the farmhouse window singing a military march already heard when sung by the troops training at Hallbach. Part of the film's complex internal aural memory, this latter piece reminds us that the world of disciplined bodies, competing nationalisms and marching feet has not been left behind but remains part of the reality that obstructs the realisation of the possibility that the farmhouse embodies.

It is in the light too of this co-existence of different possibilities that we should interpret the film's ending. It is surely no accident that Renoir had his two heroes run across virgin snow as they made their final escape (Figure 15). The snow allowed the real and the possible to be simultaneously present; the world without frontiers that had yet to be realised and the world of national divisions. Returning to the war, the heroes were running back into the past. At the same time, bearers of utopian possibility, they were moving into virgin territory, a history yet to be written, like snow on which no-one had yet trodden. Or, more complex still, the film perhaps implies that to preserve that as yet unwritten history, they would have to go back to the old one and fight, in the same way that elements of the Popular Front recognised that fascism would have to be met by force.

Pictures, windows and doors are very important to the film's timescape. Pictures accompany each prisoner on his travels. They speak of the past and the personal, of loss and separation, of spaces no longer available. They add spatio-temporal depth to the image, but they allow no passage from one time or space to another. In contrast, windows and doors allow real connection and even invite a movement through. They are thus passages where different

Figure 15: Walking into the future ... and the past?

forms of social relationship can meet and potentially spaces of transition where characters can pass from one form of existence to another.[11] Passage from the French flyers' mess to the squadron leader's office signals Maréchal's fall into history. Passage through the hatch on the castle ramparts marks Maréchal and Rosenthal's escape from the authoritarian space where they have been enclosed. Entrance into Elsa's farm signals a passage into a space where transnational relations may be reinvented. But the window that allows a German soldier to look in reminds us that other forms of social organisation have not been left behind and that different possibilities co-exist (Figure 16).

Close analysis: form and meaning

How do the issues discussed above play across some specific sequences and scenes? How do specific scenes and sequences flesh out or perhaps complicate the same issues? These are questions to which we will now turn before moving forward to a discussion of the film's politics and its problematic status as war film. If the discussion above separated the film's structure, motifs and style for the sake of analytical clarity, what follows

Figure 16: The window as meeting place of possibilities

should hopefully remind us that that separation is of course artificial, form
and content, style and meaning merging organically as they do.

I would like to begin by discussing the opening act of the film a little
more. We may remember how the set designer Lourié said that he used
the same hut for the German and French messes in a way that allowed
similarities and contrasts to emerge. To develop this point, it is worth
commenting now on how the messes are organised and shot. First the
similarities; both messes have a bar and tables that allow scenes of eating
and drinking to be staged; a record is played in each; both have walls with
posters of women and places of entertainment; both are introduced by shots
that begin with an individual by a gramophone but that then take in the rest
of the space as the camera moves.

Now the differences. The tables in the French mess are organised in a
haphazard way and occupied by small groups of men sitting in relaxed poses
(Figure 17). The hero's unwarlike desire is to go to see a woman while the
song he listens to looks back to a time before the war. The officer, when he
enters, is informal in his bearing and greeted with the similarly informal
'*tu*' address. One of the posters to which our attention is pointedly drawn
by a close-up shows an aeroplane with a slogan next to it disrespectfully
stating that alcohol kills and makes you mad and that the squadron leader
drinks it. The shot that introduces the mess, one described in detail earlier,

is a complex lateral tracking shot that moves us right then left amongst the tables creating a sense of intimacy while underscoring the haphazard organisation of the bodies and furniture in the room. The German mess has one long table around which all the occupants of the room will sit as a cohesive group. Our encounter with it begins when von Rauffenstein comes through the doorway, fresh from shooting down a plane, bringing the war in with him, even as Maréchal had sought to move away from it. Music, when it is played, comes in response to an order and as part of the celebration of the kill. The same can be said of alcohol, here drunk as a celebratory toast rather than as part of the peaceful sociability of the French mess. The shot that introduces the German mess is a long, slow track backwards that expands the visible area to show the German flyers all lined up behind each other and facing von Rauffenstein at right angles to the axis of movement of the camera (Figure 18). It is fitting of course that von Stroheim's portrayal of the aristocratic, military dandy should take centre stage here. Rather than being in amongst the informal group as in the French mess, the camera shows a formal, hierarchical group from the outside with the frontality of the shot emphasising the theatricality of what is shown. In both cases, of course, the mobile camera and composition in depth allows for the mise-en-scène of groups, with contrasts emerging from the disposition of bodies in spaces that also play an active explanatory role through their decoration and organisation. In contrast to the disrespectful poster of the French mess, the German mess has the poster of the Kaiser commented upon above with its implications of authority and respect. It also has a poster showing the Iron Cross next to a mediaeval knight, an image that obviously refers to the historical origins of the medal but also connects to the chivalrous but fundamentally outdated behaviour and self-image of Stroheim's von Rauffenstein.

The German mess shows how war and class hierarchy penetrate all areas of the group's life, including music, food and drink and bodily attitudes and dispositions. However, discussion of war in the French mess takes place in the squadron leader's office, away from where the men relax, in a way that suggests that French everyday life is less penetrated by war. It is in the same office that we see de Boeldieu for the first time. Because the aristocratic staff officer with his haughty airs is kept out of the French mess, the egalitarian and informal nature of the space is preserved. The obvious interpretation of

Figure 17: Similarities ...

Figure 18: ... and differences

the two messes would emphasise their similarities (something underlined at plot level by Maréchal's spontaneous understanding of the German mechanic and de Boeldieu's immediate bonding with the Prussian aristocrat) to suggest that they showed the unnecessary nature of war. A more subtle understanding of them would note how they played on differences and similarities. This allows them to question the setting of one nation against whilst retaining the politically necessary contrasts between hierarchy and egalitarianism, discipline and anti-authoritarianism and militarism and a reluctant acceptance of the need to fight. Rather than naively suggesting that war is simply unnecessary, the scenes hold a series of values and behaviours in tension in a way that allows peaceful co-existence to emerge as one possibility.

I would like to move next to the stables sequence that shows the English rehearsing even as the French receive a hamper of women's clothes. In typical fashion, Lourié's long, rectangular set allows both for extreme camera mobility and composition in great depth. Typically too, the sequence is introduced by a mobile long take that begins at one end of the stables with the English soldiers learning to dance like women as they sing 'It's a long way to Tipperary' and ends at the other with the French unpacking the basket of women's clothes. While unpacking, the French comment on how women's dress and hair have changed and how it must seem like one is going to bed with a boy. Maisonneuve, a particularly fresh-faced young soldier is persuaded to put on a dress. When he initially appears, the others won't look at him, wishing to hold onto the illusion of real women that the clothes have conjured up. When they turn to face him, Maréchal comments that he looks like 'a real girl'. Registering the shock that this realisation produces on everybody in the space, the sequence cuts sharply to a close-up of a soldier at the other end of the stables looking left towards the young man even as an eerie silence falls. Refusing the conventional cut-on-a-look, the camera tracks laterally past faces all looking the same way, stops and pans left to pick out Maisonneuve as, pinned by multiple eyes, he steps away from the French group and into the middle of the room. He comments, 'it's strange' his voice sounding hollow in the large, silent space (Figure 19).

One way to explain away the sequence and the eerie moment that ends it is to see it as expressing the painful sexual longing of men trapped in war and locked up in a camp. But its complexity begins to emerge when we locate it in the broader context of a film where gender destabilisation is an ongoing motif. The sequence takes this broader trend to its limits. Coupling male bodies and clothes with female gestures, the dancing Englishmen suggest a masculinity beginning to come apart. The remark about it seeming as if one were going to bed with a boy continues a process that comes to its head when Maisonneuve passes convincingly as a woman. Stable genders that

Figure 19: Unstable genders

tie gestures, clothes, appearances and desires to polarised male and female identities seem to have gone. This flux is double edged. If it connects to a nostalgia for pre-war stability first expressed when Maréchal sang 'Frou frou' and echoed here by the equally nostalgic 'It's a long way to Tipperary,' it also opens identity onto history in a way that is potentially liberating. If the war depends on the rigidly masculine, does the destabilisation of masculinity not suggest a way to move beyond it?[12]

The next scene I would like to examine is the one that shows the French in their Hallbach room as they prepare for their entertainment evening. As they work on their costumes and discuss reasons why they wish to escape, the noise of marching feet is heard in a way that brings the young Germans training in the courtyard to our attention even though we cannot see them. The marching is joined by trilling fifes, still unseen. The French are drawn to the window. A shot shows them penned into the narrow window frame, their entrapment emphasised by the two vertical window struts that further restrict their space. Although they stand tightly together they are the opposite of an organised group. Some are taller, others shorter. Only two wear uniforms. The rest wear a motley array of theatrical costumes. The schoolteacher still wears the clown's ruff that was attached to him even as he complained of his wife's infidelity (Figure 20). Although we cannot see the Germans, the music and marching feet suggest a contrasting, disciplined group. We cut to a close-up that tracks laterally to record both the rapt attention of each of the French in turn and their different explanations of the seduction of what they are hearing. While de Boeldieu attributes its power to the fifes, Maréchal, who speaks last and with most gravitas, links it to the sound of marching feet.

Figure 20: Looking into Nazi Germany?

The little segment is fascinating in a range of ways. Formally, it is an excellent example of how the film uses sound to bring off-screen space alive, connecting what we see to a broader context and bringing different groups into contact. It is also remarkable for its temporal depth and complexity, its mise-en-scène of historical possibility. On the surface, it is about the contrast between the imprisoned and their gaolers during the Great War. On a deeper level, it is also about the situation in Europe in the 1930s and about the encounter between two different modes of social organisation. Looking out of their window, the French are looking into Nazi Germany, a country seduced by the power of massed marching and uniformed spectacle. Through its choreography of bodies the extract thus helps establish the contrast between the two nations at the time of the film's making. It is also an excellent example of the reflexivity that the film repeatedly cultivates and that is an essential element of its anti-fascist politics. Because it does not show us the marching Germans but instead focuses on the French reaction, it invites the French audience of the mid-1930s to reflect on their own potential seduction by fascist order and synchronised spectacle. Whereas fascism invited fusional identification with the power of the mass, Renoir's film asks its spectators to step back and reflect.

The next passage I would like to comment on is a single fifteen second shot in the German guardroom as the soldiers celebrate the capture of Douaumont from the French. We have already watched the singing and drinking men through the window but this shot places us in the room with them. A typically mobile group shot, it begins by showing the men rejoicing with a map of their country on the wall behind them, moved by apparently spontaneous popular nationalism (Figure 21). The camera tracks left and pans right to give us a close-up of the guitarist at the centre of the group. The pan continues right to centre a pianist with his back to us in front of another wall that we cannot yet see properly. Exploiting the vertical axis that is used so tellingly in the film to bring questions of power into focus, the camera then tilts upwards to bring the wall into full view. On it we see two portraits, one of the Kaiser and one of his wife. Below them, on top of the piano are the military helmets that the singing men have removed (Figure 22). The shot is remarkable in three ways. Firstly, it chooses to align us with the celebrating Germans, inviting us to empathize with their moment of triumph, to understand the emotional power of aggressive nationalism. Secondly, it performs a wonderful piece of ideological analysis by showing how this apparently popular attachment to nation (the soldiers in front of the map) works to sustain a hierarchical social order and the militarism that goes with it (the portraits and the helmets). Thirdly, precisely through this combination of the warmly emotional and the coldly analytical, the film underlines its capacity to engage with lived experience without allowing itself to be sucked into it. The kind of spectatorship it invites is simultaneously engaged (we are placed amongst the celebrating group) and distanced (we are invited to reflect on the socio-political significance of what we see). It is easy to denounce war. It is much more useful to engage with the seduction of nationalism.

Connecting the three extracts just discussed, the famous 'Marseillaise' scene is one of the high-points of the film. The 'Marseillaise' marks the finale of an astonishingly sustained musical sequence that begins with the marching feet and fifes of the German troops and the singing of 'Die Wacht am Rhein' by the guards and continues with the performance by Cartier of

Figure 21: Nationalism from below ...

Figure 22: ... or above?

the comic love song, 'Marguerite' and by the English in drag of 'It's a long way to Tipperary'. If watching the Germans marching and singing allowed the French to view the power of nationalist spectacle and the hollowness of vicarious celebration from the outside, the 'Marseillaise' scene shows how they have failed to learn any lessons from what they have witnessed and are just as susceptible to spectacle and vicarious triumph as their foes. As if to underline this, the camera repeatedly places us amongst the audience during the concert, inviting us to share and understand their emotion. This happens in a particularly striking way when Maréchal interrupts the music to announce the recapture of Douaumont. Taking up a hitherto unused position, the camera places us at the back of the audience as they spontaneously rise to their feet looking at the luminous rectangle of the stage (Figure 23). In front of our own luminous rectangle, an extension of the on-screen public, we are invited to feel the full power of that nationalist surge before it is deflated by Maréchal's solitary confinement and the renewed loss of the fort.

Like the earlier shot in the German guardroom, but in a more extended manner, this musical sequence invites us to reflexively explore the power of spectacle and to feel its seduction. Underlining its aggressive intent, the 'Marseillaise' drives the German officers out of the shared space, even as 'Marguerite' and 'It's a long way to Tipperary' had seemed to invite them in. Sandwiched between competing nationalist anthems, the two love songs are caught, in characteristic fashion, between the utopian and the real. While they show the capacity of music (and of popular culture more generally) to transcend national frontiers, they are already a covert expression of defiance and are thus part of the very thing from which they seem to offer an escape. Their co-optation by nationalism is unmasked when one of the British officers who sang 'Tipperary' pulls of his wig to launch the singing of the 'Marseillaise'. Revealing the animosity beneath the apparent cordiality of the concert, the officer simultaneously reminds us of the virile defiance beneath the feminised surface of the performers in a way that both echoes and answers the cross-dressing scene considered above. While that earlier scene could be seen to point towards a masculine mutability that might make men less likely to fight, this one suggests that such a utopian possibility remains purely illusory as long as rival nationalisms retain their hold.

The final scene I would like to comment closely on is the one that takes place in von Rauffenstein's room as de Boeldieu lays dying. The scene is remarkable in several ways. Following the relatively fast cutting of the escape sequence, its succession of long and very long takes endows it with great solemnity and pathos. The latter quality is underscored by the justly celebrated moment when von Rauffenstein cuts the geranium, the solitary flower in the otherwise grim fortress, an act that beautifully externalises the aristocrat's

Figure 23: Watching the audience. Watching ourselves.

grief and is a suitably romantic way to mark the tragic end of his 'romance'
with the Frenchman. While these things could be commented on at greater
length, what I would like to focus on here is the scene's complex deployment
of Christian symbolism. The first time we see von Rauffenstein's chamber,
our attention is immediately drawn to a massive crucifix which dominates
the room. The same cross is also centre shot at the beginning of the scene
where the two aristocrats talk about the fate of the aristocracy (Figure 24).
Significantly, however, we do not see it in the death scene. Its place is taken
by a cluster of smaller crosses suggesting that the once unifying Christian
symbol has lost its central role and unifying power. The cluster is introduced
when one of the film's characteristic establishing close-ups of an object allows
us to see a small crucifix in a case carried by a chaplain. The same shot allows
us to see two further crosses on the chaplain's chest, one clearly religious, the
other an Iron Cross, the German military medal. As the chaplain moves away
from the camera and turns to allow von Rauffenstein to put his coat on, we
see two more crosses on him, one on a white armband that must be the red
cross worn by such as medical personnel, the other a little crucifix close to his
neck (Figure 25). The collection of crosses is rounded out by the Iron Cross
that adorns von Rauffenstein's neck and the red cross on the headdress of the
nurse tending the dying Frenchman. The competing crosses bring out the
ambiguity of modern Christianity. If the crucifix holds onto the original pan-

European religious dimension and the red cross connects to a trans-national ethic of care, the Iron Cross shows how Christianity can legitimise militarism. Typically of the film, utopian possibility (a nurturing internationalism) and the obstacle to its realisation (aggressive nationalism) are held in creative tension. The utopian dimension will only be able to come to the fore at Elsa's farm, notably in the Christmas scene, but the militarised Iron Cross draped over the portrait of Elsa's dead husband serves as a reminder that the nation's grasp will not magically vanish even there.

Other broadly contemporaneous anti-war films – to which we shall shortly come – similarly mobilise Christian iconography. Crosses by graves routinely invite us to see soldiers as Christ-like figures. Hospital scenes in adapted churches (as, for example, in Lewis Milestone's *All Quiet on the Western Front* (1930)) ask us to ponder how a supposedly Christian Europe is slaughtering its youth. *La Grande Illusion* is thus on similar terrain to other works. But its use of Christian iconography is more complex and more politically productive. If it is fully aware of the betrayal of religion and its co-optation, it also holds onto its more positive dimensions by balancing, for example, the crucifix with the crib. Other films tend not to be able to see beyond the former. *La Grande Illusion* uses the latter to keep the future open.

Misrepresenting the war?

La Grande Illusion was far from the first great anti-war film but it was certainly different from all its predecessors, as Andrew Kelly has noted.[13] We will need to ask whether this difference enabled it to engage with the war more productively or instead rendered it less able to provide an adequate representation. Before we do that, we will need to provide a sense of the anti-war cinema that preceded it. The first French contribution to the anti-war series was made by Abel Gance's *J'accuse* (1919), a film that was begun while the fighting continued and which famously used real soldiers, many soon to die, as extras.[14] The film was notable for a melodramatic plot, the use of audacious visual techniques to convey the horror of the war and an ending that saw the dead return to reproach the living with their irresponsibility. Hollywood cinema took up the anti-war mantle in the 1920s with films

Figure 24: A symbol intact ....

Figure 25: ... and in pieces

such as King Vidor's *The Big Parade* (1925) and Raoul Walsh's *What Price Glory?* (1926), both of which opposed the harsh realities of war to the hollow discourses of honour and courage that had been used to legitimise it.[15] A few years later, at the end of the silent era, Catholic nationalist director Léon Poirier would release his *Verdun, visions d'histoire* (1928), a film that, despite its mobilisation of typed characters and didactic tone, sought to recreate the murderous battle in quasi-documentary manner. Although it celebrated French courage and sacrifice, it was pacifist in intent and ended with an image of a huge graveyard covered in white crosses.[16] A reworked sound version was released in 1932.

The advent of recorded sound coincided with the release of three great films that mark the high water mark of pacifist film-making. The most famous and most widely seen of these was Milestone's *All Quiet on the Western Front*, a Hollywood, English-language adaptation of Erich Maria Remarque's great German novel. The same year, 1930, saw the release of German director, G. W. Pabst's *Westfront 1918*, another novel adaptation. The trio was completed in 1932 when prominent French director, Raymond Bernard released *Les Croix de bois* (*The Wooden Crosses*), a film version of the best-selling Raymond Dorgelès novel of 1919. If earlier films had already established some of the stereotypical iconography and landscape of the war (the trenches, the mud, the barbed war, the shell burst), these films gave it its soundscape (rifle and machine gun fire, artillery explosions, the whistle of shells before they land). They were thus able to advance a claim to realism grounded both in their complete refusal of any romantic vision of war and in the capacity of sound to restore a missing dimension to the portrayal of struggle. The way sound transformed the sensory experience of watching screened war is underlined by Pierre Sorlin:

> The sensation of the period was *All Quiet on the Western Front* (1930). The depiction of the horror of war in this movie was not very different from what could be found in previous pictures ... but there were important innovations. Violent, unrestrained, the soundtrack transformed the movie theatre into a battlefield; spectators were overwhelmed by the gun shots, the rattling of machine-guns and the whistling of bullets ...[17]

Sorlin goes on to analyse how the early 1930s films helped establish a series of clichés that would dominate representation of the war. The first cliché, predictably, was the trench. The second, the night patrol caught in barbed war and the third, the disfigured landscape with broken trunks, ruins, shell-holes and water-filled craters.[18] Sorlin finds that these clichés are usually located within a consistent narrative pattern whereby spectators are introduced to a group of characters who are all doomed to die. The end of the films, Sorlin tellingly comments, is 'like a world's end; no story can be told; there is not even any possibility of history'.[19]

Sorlin's overview is usefully complemented by an important piece by Bernd Hüppauf who writes about patterns of visual representation of the war. The core of Hüppauf's rich argument is that dominant images of the conflict were condemned to misrepresent it because they essentially functioned by opposing the human face to the destructive violence of technology. As Hüppauf notes, 'such [a] representation of modern war aims at maintaining a dichotomy between war and civilization. It is based on a concept of humanity and nature that is being eroded by the very conditions of modern civilization.'[20] Focussing on the threat of industrialised war to the human, photographic images and films failed to register the way in which the soldiers had been reduced to the status of 'appendages of anonymous, huge structures'.[21] Hüppauf helps us understand some of the limitations of the great anti-war films of the early 1930s. As both their visual texture and their soundscape revolve around the opposition between a small, human group and the inhuman forces (the deformed landscape, the destructive sounds) that threaten it, they are unable to engage with the ways in which the humans themselves are agents of destruction or conventional understandings of the human are dissolved by war.[22]

Hüppauf goes on to establish a contrast between the aerial photography so much used during the war and the heroic imagery of flyers. He suggests that aerial shots are symptomatic of 'new modes of mediated perception of battlefields made up of huge concentrations of material and masses of soldiers in a vast space that no individual would be capable of surveying.'[23] If the aerial photograph thus provides an insight into the abstract and mediated face of modern warfare, the public image of the flyer, the cult hero of the period, suggests a wilful refusal to recognise its novelty, or, rather, a way to tame this novelty by tying the new (the mechanical and technological) to the traditional (the individual hero and chivalrous combat).[24] As Hüppauf writes:

> Planes and aerial combat more than any other modern system of arms ... were considered ideal for the creation of images of heroes who, in a war of mass armies and increasing abstraction, represented the ideal of the pure knight, the strong individual and master of both nature and the machine ... In public imagination the world of aerial combat was made up of the idealised face of the young hero, images of open duels, with the space of the seconds taken by whole nations, and a reinterpretation of the empty space of aerial photography in terms of individual experience and collective mythology.[25]

A preliminary question that arises from a reading of Hüppauf and Sorlin might be whether, by avoiding the established clichés, *La Grande Illusion* perversely moved even further than other films towards the kind of outdated humanist representation of the war that made serious engagement with its novelty impossible. On the surface, the case for such a reading of the film is strong. Two of its heroes are airmen, the knights of the sky whose public image distorted perception of the war. Its characters tend to be highly individualised and in some cases charismatic in a way that suggests a failure to engage with the abstraction and dehumanisation of industrialised mass killing. Furthermore, it seems to suggest a dangerously comfortable perception of the war, with one pristine death being seen, complete with lacy sheets. While other films mentioned above show that the war was a sordid affair – one of the raw recruits in *All Quiet on the Western Front* soils his trousers on the first night patrol – *La Grande Illusion*'s war seems clean, well fed and, on the rare occasions when violence intrudes, decorously bandaged. Gance's sound version of *J'accuse* (1937) used the misshapen faces of veterans with head wounds to figure the arisen dead. Renoir's film gives us the intact good looks of Gabin and the dandyism of von Stroheim. The script, we should remember, was characterised by a progressive de-brutalisation as it reached its final state. Does the film simply sanitise the war? Perhaps not. It is simply not about the war in the same way as its illustrious predecessors. Those films had made their anti-war case by saturating their sound and image tracks with the brutalising effects of war and by figuring the impact of pain, hunger and discomfort on small groups of common soldiers. Renoir's film self-consciously avoids those effects in order to allow other things to be seen, heard and felt.

Part of the film's novelty lies in its personnel. While the other anti-war classics concentrated on common soldiers in the trenches. *La Grande Illusion* focuses on officers removed from the conflict by imprisonment. While this choice is clearly partly motivated by the Pinsard source story, it also allows the war to be held at arms length so that we will not be blinded or deafened by its overwhelming immediacy. De Boeldieu is a staff officer, Maréchal a reconnaissance pilot and Rosenthal an artilleryman. The film thus foregrounds characters who have seen the war at a distance and from a position of relative comfort. Their comfort continues within the camp where their officer status frees them from the labour forced upon other ranks and where Rosenthal's wealth insulates them from hunger.[26] Part of the fighting but also partly outside it, they effectively serve as a bridge between combatant and non-combatant experience. The other anti-war films typically opposed the soldiers to the civilians, those who knew the war to those who were ignorant of it, all to the moral advantage of the former. Avoiding this unproductive division, Renoir's film investigates the emotional investment that *all* groups make in war and nationalism. Nowhere is this clearer, of course, than in the 'musical' section where both French and German derive such a warm glow from their vicarious triumphs at the murderous battle for Verdun.

The other films ground their realism in the capacity to show the battlefield in its full horror. Taking an opposing tack, *La Grande Illusion* foregrounds the inability to see the war. This is signalled in the opening scene when de Boeldieu, Maréchal and the squadron leader examine an aerial photograph of their enemy's position. The trio cannot agree on how to interpret a line seen in the picture. Is it a road, a railway line or a disused canal? They cannot be sure. Although, unlike the soldiers on the ground, they can see the bigger, abstract picture that is an essential part of modern war, they have no experience of the immediate horror that is the soldiers' lot. One conclusion that we could draw is that those removed from the struggle cannot see it accurately, but a more productive lesson is surely that there is no one place from which modern war can be seen. By focussing too tightly on the immediacy of struggle, the other anti-war films deny themselves access to the range of vantage points needed to produce a more adequate picture.[27]

If *La Grande Illusion* points to the difficulty of *seeing* the war, it also refrains from deafening us with its noise. This is perhaps best indicated by another of those little moments that can pass unnoticed. It occurs as the German guards try to shoot de Boeldieu during the escape sequence. Von Rauffenstein seems to have resigned himself to his friend's fate and is walking sadly away. As a machine gun opens up, he again takes command and, raising his hand, brings the firing to an immediate halt, thus silencing one of the most emblematic sounds of the war. Rather than opposing the fragility of the human to the noisy power of mechanised destruction as other films did, Renoir's film instead asks us to listen to something else, in this case the conversation between two aristocrats and the single gunshot with which one fatally wounds the other. If this might seem a perverse refusal to face up to the impersonal brutality of modern war, it also allows us to hear dialogue that brings issues of class (the aristocrats' anachronistic politeness) and political choices (loyalty to military discipline or sacrifice in the name of social equality) to the fore in a way typical of the film. Films like *All Quiet on the Western Front* grounded their realism in their capacity to show the war in its full horror. This was essentially a realism of surface that sought to capture the immediate experience of combat, to look and sound the way the war had. While Renoir's film did not and could not completely reject this kind of realism (the film, as we know, was carefully documented), it was much more interested in getting behind the immediacy of the experience to the social, political and historical contexts of the war.

It would be a mistake to think, however, that Renoir simply avoids the war. It is always there but off screen. Unseen and unheard, it retains the capacity to break through the surface of the film (Figure 26). An early example of this is when the Germans are entertaining the French in their mess early in the film in a way dictated by von Rauffenstein's romanticised and chivalrous view of the conflict. The eating, drinking and the music stop as a wreath dedicated to a French airman is brought into the room, reminding us that war kills. Rather than overwhelming us with sound, as the previous wave of war cinema had, the film imposes a silence that allows us to ponder the contrast between the chivalrous illusion and the reality of death. Something similar happens in the first camp when the men are seen beginning to tunnel. The atmosphere is playful and theatrical as the old stagers put on a show for the newcomers. Maréchal indicates that he has heard something outside the window but is not sure what. Sent to investigate, the schoolteacher finds that another prisoner has been shot dead while trying to escape. The film chooses to puncture a sense that war is a game with something unseen and barely heard. At the same time, it self-reflexively underlines its characters' and audience's inability to hear and see the war accurately. Another self-reflexive puncturing occurs, of course, in the 'Marseillaise' scene when we are invited to share in the character's bellicose nationalism before the film imposes a sharp change of mood with news of defeat and with Maréchal's solitary confinement. By the time *La Grande Illusion* was made people were used to images of conflict. The association of Verdun with senseless slaughter had become a cornerstone of public memory of the war, not least because of the massive ossuary that

Figure 26: The dead, the absent, the empty chairs ... mute witnesses to the unseen violence of war

had been built on the site of Douaumont and the commemorations held there.[28] It was thus far more politically productive to repeatedly puncture the public's investment in nationalism while exploring the context of war and – something we will now consider – ways to move beyond it.

If, as Sorlin suggests, the classic anti-war films concluded with 'world's end', their main characters all dead, their capacity to look forwards was strictly limited.[29] When *La Grande Illusion* keeps two of the three main French characters alive, it is not simply a refusal to face up to the murderousness of the conflict but a determination to hold onto a sense of politico-historical possibility. By killing its aristocrat and by keeping alive its bourgeois Jew and its proletarian and by allowing the latter a brief idyll with a German peasant, the film is able to suggest how egalitarian internationalism offers a way *through* the war. If this possibility were presented, in historicist fashion, as an inevitable outcome of the conflict it would indeed be perversely utopian, but the film presents it, as we have seen, as a fragile possibility. Its historical scope – its shooting in what I have called 'deep time' – underlines the mutability of existing identities, boundaries and bonds and thus opens up a space, no matter how small for their re-imagining.

The film is also different from other anti-war films in its recognition that, never simply victims of war, its characters (and by implication its spectators), help sustain it. The film seems to lay the responsibility for the conflict partly at the door of the aristocratic old order, the career officers for whom armed service is both a duty and a *raison d'être*. But it also shows how the ordinary people are sucked into bellicose nationalism and thus bear their share of the blame. While it might be claimed that an adequate representation needed to show how, through its industrial scale and its perversion of the tools of modern civilisation, war shattered any sense we had of the human and overwhelmed any notion of individual responsibility, Renoir's film perversely does its political work by retaining a sense of humanity and individual agency. It is precisely because it keeps a sense of the human capacity for nurture, solidarity and understanding that it can see beyond the war and precisely because it maintains a sense of agency that it can face its characters and us with their and our responsibility in the face of a history made of competing possibilities.

Bazin is often seen as almost entirely apolitical. His remarks on *La Grande Illusion* suggest that he was rather more aware of politics than his reputation sometimes allows. The film's title is habitually taken to apply to the illusions of those who found grounds for optimism in the face of the war, believing it would put an end to wars or that the class reconciliation that sprung from it would outlast it. Turning conventional wisdom on its head, showing profound insight into the film's politics, Bazin writes:

> Doubtlessly we must take a higher view and give to the word 'illusion' a resolutely positive and even militant meaning. The great illusions are doubtlessly, on the one hand, the dreams which make life easier ... but they are above all the great illusion of the hatred which arbitrarily divides people that nothing really separates, not frontiers and the war that derives from them, not races, not social classes. The message of the film is therefore a counter-demonstration of the fraternity and equality of people. War, a fruit of hate and division, paradoxically revealing the falseness of all the moral frontiers inside the mind.[30]

Bazin immediately adds, 'Nonetheless, if frontiers are knocked down it is because they exist.'[31] This takes us close to the heart of the film and its capacity to find utopian possibilities within the war without denying the existence of barriers to their realisation or alternative, uglier possibilities that may also come to pass. The film is great political cinema because it invites its audience to face up to their responsibility to take part in the shaping of a world the mutability of whose outlines, divisions and inequalities the war has driven to the surface. It is a great war film not simply because it explores what sets people against each other, but because it invites us to think through and past conflict while asking us to face up to our own considerable investment in nationalism.

Notes

1   See Sesonske, Alexander, *Jean Renoir: the French Films, 1924–1939* (Cambridge, Mass., 1980), pp. 312–313.

2   The unfaithful soldier's wife is a cliché of First World War narratives. One can be found, for example, in Pabst's *Westfront 1918* (1930).

3   O'Shaughnessy, *Jean Renoir*, pp. 109–110, 116–120.

4   It is no accident that Lotte is given the Joseph figure (fashioned from a vegetable) to eat rather than the baby Jesus. Given a context in which a continent is devouring its young, the film would seem to be suggesting that it is better to sacrifice the old than those who might bring renewal, in the same way of course that the aristocratic representative of the old order, de Boeldieu, dies so that a new, egalitarian order might emerge.

5   O'Shaughnessy, *Jean Renoir*, pp. 55, 147–148.

6   Chion, Michel, *Le Complexe de Cyrano : la langue parlée dans les films français* (Paris, 2008), p. 23.

7   Crisp, *The Classic French Cinema*, pp. 400–404.

8   See Sesonske, *The French Films*, p. 314.

9   See Faulkner, *The Social Cinema of Jean Renoir*, p. 90.

10 The banal explanation of the portrait's location is the wartime Hindenburg cult. It does not of course exclude the other interpretation.

11 See Douchet, Jean, 'La fenêtre chez Jean Renoir', *Compte rendu du symposium international du cinéma* (Tokyo, 1996), pp. 8–10.

12 The sequence could also be seen as an unmasking of the disavowed core of male bonding. If the homosocial desire that inevitably lies at the heart of the male group is typically concealed by the expression of heterosexual longing, the sequence would seem to explore what happens when this outlet is no longer available. Standing at the symbolic heart of the group, the feminised, desirable male brings the disavowed into visibility under the dumbstruck eyes of his fellows.

13 Kelly, *Cinema and the Great War*, p. 101.

14 Ibid., p. 105.

15 Midkiff Debauche, Lesley. 'The United States film industry and World War One', in Paris, M. (ed.), *The First World War and Popular Cinema, 1914 to the present* (Edinburgh, 1999), pp. 152–156; Westwell, Guy, *War Cinema: Hollywood on the Front Line* (London, 2006), pp. 18–20.

16 Kelly, *Cinema and the Great War*, pp. 106–107.

17 Sorlin Pierre, 'Cinema and the Memory of the Great War' in Paris (ed.), *The First World War and Popular Cinema*, p. 18.

18 Ibid., pp. 20–21.

19 Ibid., p. 21.

20 Hüppauf, Bernd, 'Modernism and the photographic representation of war and destruction' in L. Devereaux and R. Hillman (eds), *Fields of Vision: Essays in Film Studies, Visual Anthropology and Visual Representation* (Berkeley, Los Angeles, 1995), p. 96.

21 Ibid., p. 101.

22 See also Westwell, *War Cinema*, pp. 23–24.

23 Hüppauf, Bernd, 'Modernism and the photographic representation of war and destruction', p. 106.

24 Endorsing this description of the public role of airmen, Morrow suggests that the anachronistic mythology of the aviator as heroic individual helped rally the public in the face of the slaughter of the latter part of the war, even as aerial combat itself became increasingly massified. Morrow, John H. Jnr, 'Knights of the sky: the rise of military aviation' in F. Coetzee and M. Shevin-Coetzee (eds), *Authority, Identity and the Social History of the Great War* (Oxford, 1995), pp. 316–7.

25 Hüppauf, Bernd, 'Modernism and the photographic representation of war and destruction', p. 109.

26 Abbal, Odon, *Soldats oubliés: les prisonniers de guerre français* (Paris, 2001), pp. 63–67.

27 Commenting on Pabst's *Westfront 1918*, Siegfried Kracauer wrote, 'Its fundamental weakness consists in not transgressing the limits of pacifism itself … [It] tends to demonstrate that war is intrinsically monstrous and senseless; but this indictment of war is not supported by the slightest hint of its causes, let alone any insight into them' (cited in Kelly, *Cinema and the Great War*, p. 95).

28 In July 1936, during the gestation stage of *La Grande Illusion*, veterans from all over Europe came together in a ceremony at Douaumont and swore an oath to defend the peace. Sherman, Daniel J., *The Construction of Memory in Interwar France* (Chicago, 1999), p. 312.

29 Sorlin, 'Cinema and the Memory of the Great War', p. 21,

30 Bazin, *Jean Renoir*, p. 59 (my translation).

31 Ibid., p. 59.

4 Reception

Pre-war triumph

Although *La Grande Illusion* was an overwhelming French and international, public and critical success on first release in 1937, its success was never narrowly cinematic because of its direct and obvious connection with the pressing issues of its day. Its director's known commitment to the Popular Front and proximity to the Communist Party, the film's blocked release in Nazi Germany, difficulty gaining entry into fascist Italy and endorsement by the democratic United States might suggest that its French release (on which we shall concentrate here) should have caused critical polemics. By and large (with the notable exception of the writer Céline) this was not the case. Why was this so? The obvious answer is that critics of different political (and apolitical!) persuasions were able to find what they wanted in a film that lent itself to a range of interpretations.

The review published in *Candide* by right-wing nationalist critic Jean Fayard is a good place to start. After separating Renoir and his opinions from the film he has made, Fayard is able to express overwhelming approval for the latter, grounding his judgement above all in the 'sincerity' of the film, its accurate rendition of the period in terms of costumes, language, historical references and, above all, 'human atmosphere'. Fayard is able to find this truthfulness in the film because he can read it in a way that aligns with his own nationalism. Although he can accuse Renoir the man of insulting France and preaching civil war in a public meeting, he finds that the film 'exalts what constitutes for us the essence of intelligent nationalism, the secret bond which unites all the men of a country'. Given this reading, it is unsurprising that he expresses a particular liking for passages such as the 'Marseillaise' sequence (conveniently detached from the deflation that follows it) and the heroic sacrifice of de Boeldieu. He notes that he is convinced by allegations that the film plagiarises *Kavalier Scharnhorst*, but suggests that the film should not be judged harshly for borrowing from such a sure source, one that, as we noted, renders the war in decidedly nationalist tones. He criticises, however, the last section of the film for pandering to the public, in a way the rest of the film doesn't, by allowing a feminine presence and a 'little romantic idyll'. Tellingly, he makes no mention of the internationalism embedded in the love story. He also expresses puzzlement about the need for de Boeldieu's apparent suicide, given that the aristocrat had bought his comrades time to escape.[1] The refusal to engage with the film's underlying egalitarian class politics and the historical vision associated with them is clearly significant.

One might have expected Communist dailies *L'Humanité* and *Ce Soir* to develop a doctrinaire counter-reading of the film. However, their reviews were *politically* low-key even if glowing with enthusiasm. Writing in *Ce Soir*, for which Renoir also wrote, Pierre Bonnel opened by saying, 'A great film. Finally, a work that deals with the war with a human and true tone without tawdry exaltation and without hatred.' The same sentiments could easily have found their way into Fayard's review, although 'human' and 'true' would not have meant the same thing. Bonnel's political line only begins to come through with more force when he expresses a preference for precisely that part of the film that Fayard least likes, the romantic idyll. He comments, 'After the nightmare of the camp, the world distorted by the war, it is a kind of return towards simple gestures, elemental emotions; towards that which is permanent and healthy, the very laws of life.'[2] While the lack of an *overtly* partisan interpretation of the film can be connected to the Popular Front context, a time when the Communist Party worked to reach out for the widest possible political constituency, it is nonetheless significant that Bonnel's preference goes to the most obviously internationalist part of the film while he would clearly relate Fayard's preferred nationalist parts of the film to the world 'distorted by war'. In an equally glowing review in *L'Humanité*, Louis Chéronnet similarly emphasised the internationalist idyll in the mountains with class predictably privileged over nation as a master signifier. He writes; 'Just as von Rauffenstein and de Boeldieu are from the same cast, she [Elsa] feels of the same social position as the ex-mechanic [Maréchal]. The war is not theirs. Essentially it is waged against them, against their right to happiness.' He concludes, '*La Grande Illusion* is a great human film which does honour not only to French cinema but also to the French ideology', a comment indicative of the Communists' adoption of a nationalist line during the Popular Front, the 'French ideology' referred to obviously being the republican and revolutionary tradition.[3] A more apparently neutral line can be found in a mainstream newspaper like *Paris-Midi*. Its critic, Paul Reboux, praises the film for its artistry and humanity and, echoing other critics, for an avoidance of cinematic effects and clichés that allows it to capture life. As elsewhere the cast is praised for its excellence.[4]

While the handful of newspapers considered cannot provide a rounded survey, they do give an overall sense of the response to a film that was praised uniformly for its cinematic qualities and differentially for its outlook, with it lending itself apparently equally to nationalism, depoliticising humanism and leftist internationalism. Looking back at the reception of a film he had himself reviewed in 1937, Denis Marion wrote:

> It is always fascinating to see a work of art break free from its creators' intentions, for that is doubtlessly the proof that it has won itself the autonomy of a living thing. The pacifist intentions of the scriptwriter and the director when making *La Grande Illusion* were pretty obvious at the time but, without wanting it, they managed to get the public to join in the singing of the 'Marseillaise' in 1937 – and God knows that the French weren't militaristic that year. I remember how one of the big bosses of Warner Brothers, who had gone to see the film when passing through Paris, come back bearing a judgement that now seems incomprehensible: 'Too chauvinistic'.[5]

While Marion is undoubtedly right to point out that all films are inevitably 'rewritten' at the moment of reception, he could have paid more attention to the specific ambiguity of *La Grande Illusion* that, I would suggest, building on my earlier analysis, has three main and interconnected roots. Firstly, unable to put Frontist viewpoints in the mouths of Great War characters, the film had to work at the level of the implicit, thus opening up a considerable margin of interpretative manoeuvre for the spectator. Secondly, wishing to convey the seductions of bellicose nationalism, it risked seeming to promote the very thing it sought to move beyond. Thirdly, in a way typical of its director, it grants what one might call equal dignity to its different characters, even those such as von Rauffenstein with whom it clearly disagrees. This *apparent* even-handedness makes it easy for a critic like Fayard to align himself with de Boeldieu, even though, as the extreme rightist Céline noted with fury, the representative of the old order is granted an admirable role only to announce the end of the unequal order that he embodies.[6] Taking a different line, others have connected the film's intrinsic ambiguity to the late rewrites of the text brought about by the casting of von Stroheim. The resultant expansion of the role of the two aristocrats is felt to have revealed Renoir's nostalgia for the pre-war world and disavowed fascination for the officer class with which he had rubbed shoulders before and during the conflict, complicating what was originally a more straightforward class-driven story.[7] While the nostalgia and fascination may indeed be present, it seems to me that they are never allowed to sidetrack the film's overall vision. I would instead argue that the aristocrats are very productively used to develop its understanding of historical change.

Post-war controversy

The difficult post-war reception of *La Grande Illusion* was probably predictable from the moment that the censors chose first to block its release and then to insist on cuts. Despite itself, the film seemed to connect in complex and potentially very troubling way with profoundly painful aspects of the French experience of the Second World War, Nazi occupation and French state and non-state collaboration. In August 1945, for example, the president of the censorship commission told the press, 'If *La Grande Illusion* is brought before me tomorrow, I will be forced, with enormous regret, to ban it, for it would be indecent to show this film to a public which might include people repatriated from Buchenwald or Ravensbrück.'[8] A similar fear of touching on raw post-war nerves motivated the cuts upon which re-release was made conditional in 1946. The first cut concerned the scene where Rosenthal opens a food parcel, comments that the Germans are half-starved and gives a bar of chocolate to the guard. There are so many ways that this scene could have caused offence (the privileged Jew, the underfed Germans, the over-comfortable French, the good behaviour of the prison guards), that it is not obvious what the specific reasons for censorship were. In contrast, it is not easy to see why the second cut, which concerned the German reactions of celebration and then frustration after the capture and loss of Douaumont, was made. The reasons for the third cut, the moment when Maréchal takes Elsa in his arms, were all too obvious. The image of Franco-German rapprochement and of potential 'horizontal' collaboration connected to too many painful recent memories to be tolerated. Controversy over the re-release spread into the press, with mass-circulation daily *Paris-Matin* undertaking a survey of the opinions of a range of cultural figures on the issue that began on 8 September and continued in subsequent issues.

The most famously hostile reaction came from Georges Altman, a member of the Resistance. While Renoir had produced a written preface for the film that explained that his Germans were not those of the Second World War, Altman found that some ugly aspect of the latter conflict inevitably now informed his viewing. When the film showed the French and Germans dining together, he thought of comrades tortured by the SS. When the film showed Parlo in Gabin's arms, he thought of a friend who had escaped from Buchenwald but was handed back to the SS by German peasants.[9] As Sylvie Lindeperg notes, a very different context produced profoundly different reactions to the film. While the First World War had made pacifism and internationalism eminently respectable, the experience of the Second had brought nationalism back to the fore and made pacifism seem irresponsible if not downright treacherous. *La Grande Illusion* had developed profoundly sympathetic portrayals of Germans. This once acceptable image of the 'good German' was far more problematic in 1946, not simply because of the different nature of the second conflict but also because it played into the hands of those who sought to shift German national guilt onto the shoulders of an extremist minority. In any case, images of Franco-German understanding seemed deeply unfortunate in the light of the recent shameful history of collaboration. Moreover, what had once seemed a pro-Semitic film now seemed guilty of anti-Semitic stereotyping with Maréchal's racist outburst being seen by some critics as a provocation rather than the exorcism it had once seemed to be.[10] Starting from a similar analysis of how the two different contexts generated contrasting reactions to the film, celebrated historian Marc Ferro uses response to the film in 1946 to draw out what he calls its 'latent content', something he finds to be anti-Semitic, anti-English, pro-German and defeatist, in short Vichyist and collaborationist.[11] While his point about historically shifting interpretations is obviously a sound one, the essentialist re-reading of the film through a post-Second World War lens is clearly highly suspect. Rather more productively, Lindeperg suggests that the hostility with which the film was greeted by some in 1946 was due to the way it connected to uncomfortable memories that France was unready to address.[12] Seen in this way, the problem with the film was not, for example, its anti-Semitism but the way it confronted the French with theirs at a time when there was a collective unwillingness to face up to France's role in the deportation of the Jews.

While the polemic the film unleashed was very real, there is a danger of allowing it to obscure the fact that it was once again a major box-office hit and that there were many critics who defended it. In the perceptive piece cited above, Marion underscores the anachronism of judging a film about one war in the light of events in another. Anticipating Lindeperg's analysis he suggests the French might better use the film to reflect on how their own attitudes had evolved between 1919, 1937 and 1946. He hopes that there will be some who can put aside their prejudices to re-establish contact with one of the 'summits of French film production'.[13] Taking note of the outcry surrounding the film, the *Libération* critic suggests that it is principally reproached with not showing the Germany of the SS, the Gestapo and the extermination camps, a Germany whose outline was only beginning to appear in 1937 and which Renoir could therefore not have been expected to deal with. However, the reviewer finds a continuation of the film's aristocrats in Admiral Darlan and General Rommel, figures who aligned themselves respectively with the Vichy and Nazi regimes in order to protect their caste.[14] The review is interesting in two ways. Firstly, by directing us towards what was known in 1937, it points towards a potentially valid criticism of the film, namely that its anti-fascism failed to take sufficient note of the viciousness of the phenomenon, although one might ask how far a necessarily coded anti-fascism could have been pushed before a film about the Great War slid into blatant anachronism. Secondly, through its comments on the aristocrats, it showed that the film's class-centred message was still audible in 1946. A similar conclusion can be drawn from a review by P. B. in *Drapeau Rouge* who finds that the film's class-based internationalism has not lost any of its relevance. (S)he writes, 'Frontiers are still an invention of man. The landscape remains the same. There are factories and workers' houses everywhere; there are also the palaces of capitalists.'[15] Taking a different tack, showing that the kind of humanist reading frequently made in 1937 could also still be carried out, another reviewer suggested that the film was relevant precisely because of its capacity to assert a humanity that had been in such short supply in recent times.[16]

Serene mastery?

Compared to *La Grande Illusion*'s second release, its third in 1958 was untroubled. It had just been voted one of the twelve best films ever made by an international jury of film historians. Spaak and Renoir had painstakingly put together a complete version that would be seen without the cuts of 1946. The context had shifted. Wartime sores had healed over and no longer overwrote the reception of the film. France and Germany were allies within NATO and the newly formed European Economic Community. All was set fair for the film's coronation as a 'timeless' masterpiece. By and large the press did not disappoint. The film was lauded for its formal qualities, the excellence of its cast, its 'human' truth and its intact freshness. But there was some suggestion that it belonged to another less brutal age. One critic commented; 'In the atomic age, the First World War seems almost friendly, or in any case on a human scale … It is certainly the greatest war film … before the fission of the atom.'[17] If humanist internationalism had come to dominate the understanding of the film, dissolving its politics into a bland if admirable message of universal tolerance, there were still those who held on to a class-centred analysis, such as the critic of Communist daily *L'Humanité* who noted that, while Maréchal might indeed find Elsa again, it was certain that he would never again dine with the rich banker or hunt with the nobleman.[18] Henry Magnan disrupted the general chorus of approval by reiterating earlier criticisms of the film. He first reproached it for being 'a little chauvinistic, a little naïve, a touch anti-Semitic.'[19] He later suggested that its apparent attempt to tackle anti-Semitic stereotyping actually encouraged dangerous generalisations about Jews.[20]

While it would clearly be a mistake to suggest that the film's reception was completely stabilised by its broadly consensual 'canonisation' in 1958, some of the main lines of future discussion had certainly been laid down. At the same time, the locus of debate was undergoing a double shift. With the rise of auteurist analysis in the late 1950s, driven by the young critics of *Les Cahiers du Cinéma*, attention increasingly centred on Renoir's work as a whole rather than individual films. As part of the same process, the interesting arguments tended to be found in longer articles or in books devoted to the film-maker rather than in the press. Consistent with their auteurism and its tendency to flatten differences between films by the same director, the *Cahiers* critics, partly supported by Bazin but also by other voices, promoted a vision of Renoir as a tolerant humanist in a way that actively depoliticised his films from the Popular Front era, including of course *La Grande Illusion*.[21] Renoir himself abetted this process. While his post-war films still retained a sharply critical edge that should in itself make us distrust the easy stereotype of the epicurean, all-tolerant, humanist director, they were definitely not committed cinema. They could thus be used along with Renoir's pre-Frontist works and Hollywood films to flatten out the specificity of his Frontist period. In interviews given to *Cahiers* and elsewhere and in his own writings Renoir at least partly went along with this depoliticisation.[22] Other voices opposed this process and sought to reassert the political dimension of the Frontist works, re-reading history and class back into them. When a new wave of political cinema burst onto the scene following the rebellions and strikes of 1968, Renoir's committed films again became an essential reference, one worth defending from the auteurists.[23] Of course not all leftists took the same position or embraced Renoir's committed films uniformly. In a way reminiscent of what had happened to *La Grande Illusion* in 1946, some went back to the Frontist films and sought out signs of an already reactionary Renoir beneath the progressive surface. *La Grande Illusion* easily became a component of such analyses because earlier accounts of it had accused it of nostalgia, nationalism and anti-Semitism or had suggested that its real affections lay with the two aristocrats to whom it gave such a privileged place.[24]

Anti-Semitism?

The accusation of anti-Semitism is worth pausing on. If one were to seek to base it on the way the film was received in 1937, it certainly would not stick. The film's intention was clearly to lance the anti-Semitic boil by deliberately giving a stereotypically Jewish character a positive and central role in its egalitarian narrative and by forcing the common Frenchman, in the guise of Maréchal, to confront and overcome his own prejudice. Two notorious anti-Semites of the period certainly saw it that way. Writing in the extreme nationalist *Action Française* under the pseudonym of François Vinneuil, Lucien Rebatet recognises that Rosenthal has been given a positive role as a brave soldier but claims that the French public would be fully aware of his exceptional nature because there were too few brave Jews.[25] Characteristically vitriolic and obscene, novelist Céline also sees Rosenthal as a profoundly pro-Semitic role. He first claims that the cinema industry, notably Hollywood, is controlled by Jews and routinely pumps out covert Jewish propaganda under the mask of universalist and democratic values in order to persuade non-Jews to abandon their national and racial traditions.[26] Narrowing his sights, he then suggests that *La Grande Illusion* represents something new, the moment when, casting off its mask, Jewish propaganda becomes overt and can show a character clearly marked out as a Jew in an admirable light. He notes that the film initially seems to stack all the usual stereotypes against Rosenthal but then turns him into a positive character, advocating an alliance between him and the proletarian Maréchal, even as the traditional elite, the aristocracy, is made to will its own self-abolition.[27] Even though he clearly detested it, Céline had a clear-sighted sense of the film's politics.

It would only be later, from 1946 onwards, that the accusation of anti-Semitism would cast a shadow on the film. Two articles from the 1980s illustrate how the shadow lingered. In one, Sorlin writes, 'Rosenthal is meant to demonstrate that a Jew is not different from other Frenchmen. This point is elaborately made by the dialogue but is denied by the story which makes it clear that Rosenthal is stuck between two worlds, France and Germany (sic), at rest in neither.'[28] On not dissimilar lines, R. M. Friedman concluded; 'Renoir without doubt wanted to show the inanity of anti-Semitic prejudices by showing on the screen a generous Jewish officer. But certain clues in the dialogue and, more especially, in the visual treatment, reveal the superficial character of Renoir's liberal attitude.'[29] Renoir's unfortunate attempts to curry favour with the anti-Semitic Vichy regime before he left France for American exile might seem to provide retrospective confirmation of his latent prejudices.[30]

A very useful corrective has been provided more recently by Maurice Samuels who, after detailing the case against Renoir, mounts a persuasive defence. Samuels notes that the film tends to stereotype other characters, not only the Jewish one, but then allows them to transcend their stereotyping. De Boeldieu, for example, is heavily marked as an aristocrat by a range of features but ultimately plays a profoundly positive role through his self-sacrifice and courage. Rosenthal similarly transcends his stereotype by showing his generosity, commitment to the group and bravery. The latter quality underlines his quality as a soldier, something far from insignificant in a country where Dreyfus, a Jewish army officer, had been falsely and very famously convicted of treason due to anti-Semitic prejudice. Moreover, Rosenthal is far more integrated into the group than the aristocrat. It is with him that Maréchal, the ordinary Frenchman, chooses to escape.[31] Overall, rather than promoting a closed, ethnic view of national identity, the film offers 'a different model of Frenchness – one based not on a deterministic model of ancestry but on an affirmation of shared values and patriotic acts, one that explicitly includes the Jew.'[32] While fully endorsing Samuels' conclusion that Renoir's use of stereotyping is strategic, I prefer to conclude by replacing Rosenthal within the film's egalitarian *internationalism*. If the character is indeed used to assert an open view of nation in a way consonant with the Popular Front's attempt to wrest the national away from the right, he also plays a key role in the film's systematic questioning of boundaries and fixed identities. Speaking French and German, being Jewish but also Jesus's 'racial' brother, born in Vienna of Danish and Polish parentage, he starts out from the border-free zone that Maréchal only reaches in the later part of the film. Of course, this Jewish 'rootlessness' can easily be reclaimed by negative stereotyping, but that is far from the way the film uses it.

Notes

1   Fayard, Jean, 'La Grande Illusion', Candide, 17 June 1937.
2   Bonnel, Pierre, 'La Grande Illusion au Marivaux', Ce Soir, 12 June 1937.
3   Chéronnet, Louis, 'La Grande Illusion', L'Humanité, 16 June 1937.
4   Reboux, Paul, 'La Grande Illusion; un film admirable qu'il faut aller voir!', Paris-Midi, 13 June 1937.
5   Marion, Denis, 'La Grande Illusion', Combat, 28 August 1946.
6   Céline, Louis-Ferdinand, Bagatelles pour un massacre (Paris, 1937), pp. 166–167.
7   See Ferro, Marc Cinéma et Histoire, (Paris, 1993), pp. 185–186.
8   Cited in Lindeperg, Sylvie, Les Ecrans de l'ombre: la seconde guerre mondiale dans le cinéma français (1944–1969) (Paris, CNRS Editions), 1997, p. 210 (my translation).
9   Altman, Georges, 'La Grande Illusion', L'Ecran français, 62 (4 September 1946), p. 5.
10 Lindeperg, Les Ecrans de l'ombre, pp. 214–220.
11 Ferro, Marc, Cinéma et Histoire, (Paris, 1993), pp. 184–190.
12 Lindeperg, Les Ecrans de l'ombre, p. 219.
13 Marion, 'La Grande Illusion'.
14 Anon., 'La Grande Illusion', Libération, 7 September 1946.
15 P. B., 'La Grande Illusion', Drapeau Rouge, 24 September 1946.
16 Narce, Eric, 'La Grande Illusion', Paroles Françaises, 7 September 1946.
17 Ciantar, Maurice, 'La Dernière Chevalerie', Paris Jour, 23 October 1958.
18 Deltour, Jacques, L'Humanité, 10 October 1958.
19 Magnan, Henry, Le Canard Enchaîné, 8 October 1958.
20 Magnan, Henry, Combat, 18 October 1958.
21 See, for example, Schérer, Maurice (Eric Rohmer), 'Renoir Américain', Cahiers du Cinéma 2: 8 (1952), pp. 33–40. Rohmer suggests that, were he so minded, he could clearly reveal the signs of Renoir's later calm serenity in his apparently radical films.
22 See the collection of interviews in Renoir, Jean, Renoir on Renoir (Cambridge, 1989) (translation by C. Volk).
23 See Poulle, François, Renoir 1938 ou Jean Renoir pour rien? (Paris, 1969). See also the writings gathered together by Claude Gauteur in Renoir, Jean, Ecrits, 1926–1971 (Paris, 1974) which deliberately brings Renoir's committed journalism of the 1930s back into visibility.
24 See Chardère, Bernard (ed.), Premier Plan 22–24 (May 1962, Special Jean Renoir number), especially Oms, Marcel, 'Renoir revu et rectifié', pp. 22–24, 44–51. Oms sees La Grande Illusion as a fundamentally nationalist film which ends with an escapist and reactionary return to the land.
25 Rebatet, Lucien cit. Lindeperg, Les Ecrans de l'ombre, p. 212.
26 Céline, Bagatelles pour un massacre, p. 138.
27 Ibid., pp. 164–8.
28 Sorlin, Pierre, 'Jewish images in the French Cinema of the 1930s', Historical Journal of Film, Radio and Television, 1 / 2 (1981), p. 148.
29 Friedman, R. M., 'Exorcising the past: Jewish figures in contemporary films', Journal of Contemporary History, 19: 3, July 1984, p. 513.

30 See LoBianco and Thompson, *Jean Renoir, Letters*, pp. 75–77 and Bertin-Maghit, Jean-Pierre, *Le Cinéma français sous l'Occupation : le monde du cinéma français de 1940 à 1946*, (Paris, 1989), pp. 42–43 and 344–348.

31 Samuels, Maurice, 'Renoir's *La Grande Illusion* and the "Jewish question"', in *Historical Reflections*, 32 : 1, pp. 165–92.

32 Ibid., p. 187.

Conclusion

There are some compelling reasons why we should watch *La Grande Illusion*. I will mention just three. The first, not the least, is that it is a great film made by a supreme film-maker at the very height of his powers, seconded by a wonderful cast and creative team. The second, sufficient in itself to make the film compulsory viewing, is its intervention in the war film genre. If many films set out to show us, well or badly, how monstrous war is, they often limit themselves to that, unable to look (or hear) beyond the horror and spectacle of combat. Holding combat at arms length, *La Grande Illusion* shows that a film can examine the causes of conflict and people's investment in aggressive nationalism and yet see beyond war, on condition of course that pacifism is attached to a progressive political project. The third thing that makes the film essential viewing is that it is an essential example of political cinema, one that very usefully reminds us that progressive film can be both entertaining and challenging, accessible and remarkably intelligent in the right hands, providing that the audience is available and that popular forms can be reworked from within by a progressive vision. Through its capacity to pick up established star personas or popular songs and put them in the service of its politics, *La Grande Illusion* is exemplary in this respect. Part wartime escape drama, part romance, it is always entertaining but it is also astonishingly rigorous in its working through of what divides and unites people. Its ability to engage and move us and yet at the same time push us to examine our response to spectacle and where it may lead us is remarkable. So too is its capacity to marry form and content. Its breathtaking camera mobility, complex composition in depth, mobilisation of off-screen space and use of on- and off-screen sound are all things of beauty in themselves. But their resonance is far greater when we consider how powerfully they work to convey a vision of social relations and political potential by locating interactions in a broader context, by bringing classes and nations into contact and by showing competing historical possibilities as they vie for screen space.

If there are overwhelming reasons why we should watch the film, a vital question that still remains is how it speaks to us now. This time, one might put forward two answers. Firstly, taking inspiration from the film's remarkable reception history, its capacity to lend itself to radically opposed readings, one might adopt an easy relativism and suggest that it can mean whatever we choose to make of it at a particular historical moment. Thus, reworking the film for current fashions, we could see it as essentially about tolerance of difference, shrinking its egalitarian internationalism to the dimensions of contemporary, consensual multiculturalism, putting its pacifism in the service of pacification while conveniently forgetting its radicalism. Alternatively, getting closer to its heart, we could hold on to its capacity to challenge. *La Grande Illusion* is not simply about respect for others. It is about the mutability of the existing order, its capacity to change for better or for worse. Because existing identities are predominantly built inside current social and national boundaries, with their inevitable lot of exclusions and inequalities, any reduction of the film's message to a tolerance of others' identities is inevitably a betrayal of its radicalism. If the film is indeed about moving beyond war, it is about doing so by moving away from relations of hierarchy and domination. Its message of fraternity can only be properly heard if we remember that it is inseparable from its affirmation of equality.

La Grande Illusion is such a beautifully made film that it is tempting to think that it could only ever have been the way that it is. Our examination of its genesis, from the original Pinsard outline, discussed for the first time here, through the different drafts, to the finished work, has underscored how it was shaped by factors that included its production context, its director's progressive politicisation, a range of creative inputs and an evolving historical context. While the director's alignment with the Popular Front surely made it inevitable that a story that potentially lent itself to nationalist hagiography would mutate into something much more progressive, the film was also inflected by key creative personnel such as Spaak, Lourié and Matras (the cinematographer) and by the personas and influence of stars such as Gabin, Stroheim, Dalio and Parlo, all of whom contributed in their different ways to the form it finally took. *La Grande Illusion* refuses to privilege the individual over the group or the context. Taking our cue from it, we should remember that what is too easily seen as a work of individual genius is a collective product that responded to a specific historical moment. If we are not simply to freeze the film as a timeless classic, the challenge now is to make it speak to our time without forgetting how it spoke to its own era.

Appendix 1: Renoir's films

Catherine (*Une vie sans joie*), 1924/1927
La Fille de l'eau, 1924
Nana, 1926
Charleston (*Sur un air de Charleston*), 1927
Marquitta, 1927
La Petite Marchande d'allumettes, 1928
Tire-au-flanc, 1928
Le Tournoi, 1929
Le Bled, 1929
On purge bébé, 1931
La Chienne, 1931
La Nuit du carrefour, 1932
Boudu sauvé des eaux, 1932
Chotard et cie, 1933
Madame Bovary, 1934
Toni, 1935
Le Crime de Monsieur Lange, 1935
La Vie est à nous, 1936
Partie de campagne, 1936 (released 1946)
Les Bas-fonds, 1937
La Grande Illusion, 1937
La Marseillaise, 1938
La Bête humaine, 1938
La Règle du jeu, 1939
Swamp Water, 1941
This Land is Mine, 1943
Salute to France, 1944

The Southerner, 1945
The Diary of a Chambermaid, 1946
The Woman on the Beach, 1948
The River, 1950
The Golden Coach, 1953
French Cancan, 1955
Elena et les hommes, 1956
Le Déjeuner sur l'herbe, 1959
Le Testament du Docteur Cordelier, 1959
Le Caporal Epinglé, 1962
Le Petit Théâtre de Jean Renoir, 1969

Appendix 2: Cast and creative personnel

Jean Gabin (Lieutenant Maréchal)
Marcel Dalio (Lieutenant Rosenthal)
Pierre Fresnay (Capitaine de Boeldieu)
Erich von Stroheim (Captain, later Commandant von Rauffenstein)
Dita Parlo (Elsa)
Julien Carette (Cartier, the actor)
Gaston Modot (Cadastrial engineer)
Jean Dasté (Primary school teacher)
Werner Florian (Arthur)
Sylvain Itkine (Lieutenant Demolder)
Georges Péclet (Charpentier)
Habib Benglia (the Senegalese)
Claude Sainval (Capitaine Ringis)
Roger Forster (Maisonneuve)
Jacques Becker (English officer who breaks watch)
Carl Koch

Director: Jean Renoir. Script and dialogue: Charles Spaak and Jean Renoir. Assistant director: Jacques Becker. Technical advisor: Carl Koch. Script: Françoise Giroud (Gourdji). Set design: Eugène Lourié.

Costumes: René Decrais. Wardrobe: Suzy Berton. Make-up; Raffels. Props: Alexandre Laurié, Raymod Pillon. Cinematography: Christian Matras. Camera: Claude Renoir. Assistant cameramen: Jean-Serge Bourgoin, Ernest Boureaud. Sound engineer: Joseph de Bretagne. Original score: Joseph Kosma. Editing: Marguerite Houlle-Renoir. Director of Production:

Raymond Blondy. Producers: Frank Rollmer, Albert Pinkévitch. Distribution: Réalisations d'art cinématographiques (RAC).

Appendix 3: The evolving script

The table on the following page shows the film's evolution from the initial outline (*Les Evasions du Colonel Pinsard*), through the three previously known drafts, to the completed work. The table summarises the Pinsard outline, the first draft proper and the completed film (in the first, second and fourth columns respectively) but only lists the major changes made by the second and third drafts (in the third column).

The initial Pinsard outline	The first draft proper	Major changes and additions in the second and third drafts of the script	The film
Pinsard and lieutenant 'X' fly on a reconnaissance mission and are forced to land behind German lines by mechanical failure.	An aristocratic officer of Boeldieu is flown on a reconnaissance mission by the proletarian Maréchal. The plane is forced to land behind German lines by engine failure.	'Frou frou' is heard in the French mess. Maréchal is about to go and see Joséphine. The two Frenchmen are shot down. Along with the German pilot who has landed beside them, they see another German plane shot down.	An aristocratic officer de Boeldieu is flown on a reconnaissance mission by the proletarian Maréchal. The plane is shot down behind German lines by von Rauffenstein, the German squadron leader
Having failed to set light to their downed plane, the two are beaten by German troops but rescued by a German officer and invited to dine with a general and his staff in their château headquarters.	Having successfully set light to their downed plane, the two are beaten by German troops but rescued by a German officer and invited to dine with a general and his staff in their château headquarters. The officer, his staff and de Boeldieu speak in English. Maréchal's neighbour has worked at the Gnôme plant at Lyon. The two converse in French about shared interests.	The two Frenchmen are now invited to eat with the German squadron leader (von der Winter) and his men in their mess hut.	The two Frenchmen are invited to dine with von Rauffenstein and his men in their mess hut. Rauffenstein and de Boeldieu speak in English. Maréchal's neighbour has worked at the Gnôme plant at Lyon. The two converse in French about shared interests.
Pinsard and 'X' are separated. Pinsard finds himself in a camp where he shares a room with French, Belgian, English and Russian officers. Two officers attempt to escape by hiding in a rubbish cart but are caught because a young typist has seen their preparations. A second attempt using a tunnel also fails when the men are betrayed by a Russian who is jealous because a woman worker has fallen for Pinsard!	Both prisoners are transferred to a camp and are lodged in a room where four other officers have been preparing an escape tunnel. All except de Boeldieu are simple men and mix easily, with the implication being that they are now all French. One is a bank robber with pre-war experience of tunnelling!	A sequence on a train is incorporated. The officers in the room in the first camp now include an actor, a teacher, an engineer and a Jew, sometimes explicitly named as Rosenthal, who by draft three is feeding the others.	Both prisoners are transferred to a camp and are lodged in a room where four other officers have been preparing an escape tunnel. All except de Boeldieu are simple men and mix easily. Rosenthal provides food for the other men.

The initial Pinsard outline	The first draft proper	Major changes and additions in the second and third drafts of the script	The film
	The old hands tell the new arrivals about German women workers on the same site and how one deliberately reattaches her suspenders by the prisoners' basement window to torment the men.	The subplot with the provocative German woman remains in drafts two and three.	
	The men are preparing a theatre show making use of dresses and costumes sent from Paris by couturiers. The Germans celebrate the capture of Douaumont by singing. The French go on with the show. During the performance, told by Maréchal of the recapture of the fort, they spontaneously burst into a defiant 'Marseillaise' and dance wildly, provoking a violent intervention from the guards		The men are preparing a theatre show making use of dresses and costumes sent from Paris by Rosenthal's family. The Germans celebrate the capture of Douaumont by singing. The French go on with the show. During the performance, told by Maréchal of the recapture of the fort, they spontaneously burst into a defiant but dignified 'Marseillaise'. The guard's intervention is implied but not seen.
Following the failed escape attempt, Pinsard is thrown into solitary confinement. He cannot bear the isolation, wants to kill himself and is saved by the kindness of an old German guard who calms him by allowing him to read letters that have been sent to him.	Maréchal is thrown into solitary confinement for his insolence, cannot bear the isolation, loses control, wants to kill himself and is calmed down due to the kindness of an old guard		Maréchal is thrown into solitary confinement for his insolence, cannot bear the isolation, loses control and is calmed down due to the kindness of an old guard who gives him a mouth organ to play.
After his release, Pinsard has to be helped to his room by the guards. His comrades cry when they realise the state he is in.	After Maréchal's release, the men decide to revenge themselves on the German woman who torments them with the sight of her legs and stockings. They pull her leg through the window bars, tear off her stocking and Maréchal bites her bare flesh.	In the third draft, when the men grab the German woman, she shouts to them that Douaumont has been recaptured by the Germans.	After Maréchal's release, Rosenthal cries when he sees the state he is in.

The initial Pinsard outline	The first draft proper	Major changes and additions in the second and third drafts of the script	The film
	Just when the tunnel is ready, the prisoners are transferred. Maréchal attempts to tell newly arriving English prisoners about the tunnel but fails to communicate. The English are shown starting a new tunnel five metres from the first one.		Just when the tunnel is ready, the prisoners are transferred. Maréchal attempts to tell newly arriving English prisoners about the tunnel but fails to communicate.
A conversation between the commandant and Pinsard reveals that the latter has made several more escape attempts. He is to be transferred to the Ingolstadt fortress in Bavaria.	The men are moved to a second, austere camp in a mediaeval castle.		The men are moved to a second, austere camp in Wintersborn, a mediaeval castle.
		In draft two, the German commandant makes a speech about the difficulty of escape from the fortress camp. In draft three, the same figure lists the different escapes made by the transferred men.	A conversation between the commandant, Maréchal and de Boeldieu reveals that both have made multiple escape attempts. The commandant takes the new arrivals on a tour of the castle.
Pinsard is reunited with 'X', his observer. In the camp, there is a Parisian proletarian called Claude, who amuses the others and feeds them with food stolen from confiscated parcels.	The prisoners' room contains a Greek teacher translating a classical poet, a polite, reserved Black prisoner and a locksmith. De Boeldieu finds another French prisoner of his own class. Maréchal connects with another prisoner, an intellectual called Dolette. There is a cheeky Parisian whose humour no longer amuses anyone.	Dolette remains in both drafts, as does the locksmith.	The prisoners' room contains a Greek teacher translating a classical poet and a polite, reserved Black prisoner. Maréchal is reunited with Rosenthal. De Boeldieu is brought back together with von Rauffenstein, a German of his own class. The two will have a long conversation about the fate of the European aristocracy.

The initial Pinsard outline	The first draft proper	Major changes and additions in the second and third drafts of the script	The film
	A rebellious little Breton is sent to solitary for repeatedly insulting the German guards. The Parisian cries on seeing his state when he is returned to the group.	The Russian prisoners are introduced. By draft three, the sequence where they create chaos by burning a crate of books is developed.	Russian inmates receive a crate that they think contains food. Learning it contains books, they burn it, causing chaos.
Pinsard escapes with 'X'. Claude helps mask the escape by leading the prisoners in singing the 'Marseillaise', using the French recapture of the fort of Douaumont as a pretext. A cavalry lieutenant loses his life delaying the pursuers, as do Claude and some others. Claude is shot after climbing onto the roof.	Maréchal escapes with Dolette. De Boeldieu and the humorous Parisian create a diversion by provoking and striking guards. They escape to a roof. The Guards open fire. Both men are killed.	When Maréchal and Dolette escape, it is now only de Boeldieu who sacrifices himself. Shot whilst on the roof, de Boeldieu falls into the yard and dies quickly.	Maréchal escapes with Rosenthal. The prisoners collectively organise a diversion. De Boeldieu distracts the guards and is shot having climbed on a roof.
Pinsard and 'X' hide by day and walk by night with only some biscuits and sugar to feed themselves.	Maréchal and Dolette have only some biscuits and sugar to feed themselves. They hide by day and walk by night. The pair are nearly captured by German reservists who sing as they march on a forest road.	The two escapees are pursued by dogs and have to hide under sticks to avoid capture.	Maréchal and Rosenthal have only biscuits and sugar to feed themselves. They hide by day and walk by night.
'X' has sprained his foot and can barely walk. Following customary practice, and by mutual accord, Pinsard leaves his injured friend, only to return for him later.	Dolette has hurt his foot and can barely walk. He tells Maréchal to leave him. Maréchal will not desert his friend.	In drafts two and three, the injured Dolette tells Maréchal that he must go on. Dolette sings 'Il était un petit navire'. Maréchal leaves him but returns.	Rosenthal has hurt his foot and can barely walk. Maréchal temporarily abandons him after an Anti-Semitic outburst.

The initial Pinsard outline	The first draft proper	Major changes and additions in the second and third drafts of the script	The film
	The two hide in a shed and are surprised there by a blonde German woman. Starved of male company she sleeps with Maréchal and Dolette.	Elsa is present in drafts two and three. In draft three, the young German reservists knock on Elsa's shutters as they march past. The Christmas sequence is largely in place. Lotte already wants to eat baby Jesus.	The two hide in a shed and are surprised there by Elsa, a blonde German woman. She shelters them in her home, keeping their presence hidden from some German reservists who sing as they march past her farmhouse. Elsa and Maréchal fall in love.
	The two are forced to kill a German guard to cross the border. Once over it, they steal bread from a young Swiss girl.	In draft two, they still steal bread from a little Swiss girl. In draft three, they no longer do so. In the same draft, the old border guard is tied up rather than shot.	The two cross the border but are then fired upon by some border guards who, realizing they are in Switzerland, let them go on their way.
The two reach the border but cannot bring themselves to kill a German guard. They are able to cross to when the guard answers a call of nature. Exhausted, they quarrel bitterly, with Pinsard complaining of the stench of his comrade's injured foot. They eat in a station buffet, catch a train to Geneva and are smuggled over the French border by the French consul.		Draft two ends with the scene at Maxim's: Maréchal arrives but Dolette does not. Draft three ends when, safely over the border, the two are surrounded by Swiss guards. The two men sing 'Il était un petit navire.'	The film ends with Maréchal and Rosenthal walking in the snow just over the Swiss border.
An epilogue shows a reserved but empty table at Maxim's restaurant in Paris on 25th December 1918. The two had promised to meet there to celebrate Christmas but are nowhere to be seen.			
Closing subtitles recount Pinsard's heroic exploits as wartime ace and post-war role training pilots.			

Appendix 4: Select bibliography

Bazin, André, *Jean Renoir* (Paris, 1989).

Bergan, Ronald, *Jean Renoir: Projections of Paradise* (London, 1992).

Bergfelder, Tim, Harris, Sue and Street, Sarah, *Film Architecture and the Transnational Imagination: Set Design in 1930s European Cinema* (Amsterdam, 2007).

Crisp, Colin, *The Classic French Cinema, 1930–1960* (Bloomington, Indiana, 1997).

Curchod, Olivier, *La Grande Illusion* (Paris, 2005).

Curchod, Olivier and Faulkner, Christopher, *La Règle du jeu: scénario original de Jean Renoir* (Paris, 1999).

Dalio, Marcel, *Mes années folles* (Paris, 1976).

Faulkner, Christopher, *The Social Cinema of Jean Renoir* (Princeton, 1986).

Ferro, Marc, *Cinéma et Histoire*, (Paris, 1993).

Hüppauf, Bernd, 'Modernism and the photographic representation of war and destruction' in L. Devereaux and R. Hillman (eds), *Fields of Vision: Essays in Film Studies, Visual Anthropology and Visual Representation* (Berkeley, Los Angeles, 1995).

Kelly, Andrew, *Cinema and the Great War* (London, 1997).

Lindeperg, Sylvie, *Les Ecrans de l'ombre: la seconde guerre mondiale dans le cinéma français (1944-1969)* (Paris, 1997).

LoBianco, Lorraine and Thompson, David (eds). *Jean Renoir, Letters* (London, 1994), (translations by C. Carlson, N. Arnoldi and M. Wells).

Lourié, Eugène, *My Work in Films* (San Diego, 1985).

Luzzatto, Sergio, *L'Impôt du sang: la gauche française à l'épreuve de la guerre mondiale 1900–1945* (Lyon, 1996).

Oms, Marcel, 'Renoir revu et rectifié', pp. 22–51 in Chardère, Bernard (ed.), *Premier Plan 22-24* (May 1962, Special Jean Renoir number).

O'Shaughnessy, Martin, *Jean Renoir* (Manchester, 2000).

O'Shaughnessy, Martin, 'La Règle du Jeu', in P. Powrie (ed.), *The Cinema of France* (London, 2004), pp. 40–49.

Paris, M. (ed.), *The First World War and Popular Cinema, 1914 to the present* (Edinburgh, 1999).

Poulle, François, *Renoir 1938 ou Jean Renoir pour rien?* (Paris, 1969).

Priot, Franck (ed.), *La Grande Illusion: le film d'un siècle* (special number), *Archives* 70 (February 1997).

Prost, Antoine and Winter, Jay, *Penser la Grande Guerre: un essai d'historiographie* (Paris, 2004).

Renoir, Jean, *Ecrits, 1926–1971* (Paris, 1974).

Renoir, Jean, *Ma Vie et mes films* (Paris, 1974).

Samuels, Maurice, 'Renoir's *La Grande Illusion* and the "Jewish question"', in *Historical Reflections*, 32:1, pp. 165–192.

Sesonske, Alexander, *Jean Renoir: the French Films, 1924–1939* (Cambridge, Mass., 1980).

Sorlin Pierre, 'Cinema and the Memory of the Great War' in Paris (ed.), *The First World War and Popular Cinema, 1914 to the present* (Edinburgh, 1999), pp. 5-25.

Sorlin, Pierre, 'Jewish images in the French cinema of the 1930s', *Historical Journal of Film, Radio and Television* 1/2 (1981), pp. 139–150.

Vincendeau, Ginette, *Stars and Stardom in French Cinema* (London, 2000).